Bowling Green State University 1910-2010

A Legacy of Excellence

Text by
GARY R. HESS

BOWLING GREEN STATE UNIVERSITY | 1910-2010

To the BGSU History Department senior faculty of the mid-1960s, to Bill Rock and to the memories of Stuart Givens, Jack Oglevee, Grover Platt, Virginia Platt and Bob Twyman, who were all dedicated to the well-being of their students and the University and whom I, as a junior faculty member, was privileged to know as colleagues.

> Gary R. Hess

Photos provided by BGSU Center for Archival Collections and BGSU Marketing and Communications.

The Donning Company Publishers
184 Business Park Drive, Suite 206
Virginia Beach, VA 23462

Bowling Green State University
Office of Marketing and Communications
504 Administration Building
Bowling Green, Ohio 43403-0102

Jeffrey S. Artz, *Creative Director*
Julia Carle, *Editor*
BGSU UniGraphics; Paul Obringer, *Director*
and Deanna Falk, *Graphic Designer*

Library of Congress Cataloging-in-Publication Data

Hess, Gary R.
 Bowling Green State University, 1910-2010 / Gary R. Hess.
  p. cm.
 ISBN 978-1-57864-650-0
 1. Bowling Green State University--History. I. Title.
 LD4191.O62H47 2010
 378.771'16--dc22

2010034492

Printed in the United States of America by Walsworth Publishing Company

Contents

Preface

In the spring of 2005, Sidney Ribeau invited me to write the University's 100th anniversary history. I was honored and remain grateful to him for the trust inherent in that invitation.

In undertaking this project, I benefited from the two earlier official histories, which were written by longtime faculty members in conjunction with the 50th and 75th anniversaries: James Robert Overman, *The History of Bowling Green State University* (1967) and Stuart Givens, *The Falcon Soars, Bowling Green State University: The Years of Growing Distinction, 1963-1985* (1985). In addition, the earliest comprehensive history—the unpublished doctoral dissertation of Kenneth McFall, "From Normal College to University: The Development of Bowling Green State University" (Case Western Reserve University, 1947), provides much information on the 1910-1935 period.

In organizing the history, I have divided it into approximate quarter-centuries, with chapters largely following those divisions. Thus the first chapter covers the period from 1910-1935 when, under the leadership of Homer B. Williams, the normal college of 1910 evolved into a state college in 1929, and ultimately to a state university in 1935. The second chapter traces the uneven fulfillment of the University mission between 1935 and 1961, as the Great Depression, World War II and the postwar student boom established other priorities. It was not until the 1950s that the University, during the presidency of Ralph McDonald, shed its "teachers college" origins and developed into a university in practice as well as name, a process that culminated in the establishment of the first doctoral program.

The year 1961 was, in ways that McDonald never intended, a defining moment in the University's history, for during a tumultuous three months that spring, student and faculty protests against his policies, combined with McDonald's miscalculations and intervention by the Ohio General Assembly, led to McDonald's resignation. This was a turning point in the development of a system of faculty governance and the liberalization of rules affecting student life. How to deal with this controversy or "revolution" was a difficult decision. Overman's history, written shortly after the event, treated it briefly and cautiously (not mentioning the names of prominent figures) and with obvious sympathy for McDonald. Givens's book picked up the University history in 1963, and barely mentioned the "disarray" of 1961. Reflective of the ongoing interest in the controversy are several written accounts, including a 40th anniversary series of articles in the *Bowling Green Sentinel-Tribune*; as well as unpublished papers: Jim Gordon, "The One-Hundred Days of Bowling Green, March 26–June 26, 1961" (1965) which traces the extensive newspaper coverage; Joseph B. Perry, Norbert Wiley, Richard Carpenter, "The 1961 Bowling Green State University Demonstrations: How The Students Won," (ca. 2001); [anon.] "Bowling Green 1961" (ca. 2000); as well as some student papers on different aspects of the controversy.

As I delved into the rich materials in the Center for Archival Collections at William T. Jerome Library, it became clear that this story could not be told adequately in just a few pages at the end of chapter 2. With input from the University History Advisory Committee, I decided to devote chapter 3 to the McDonald story because of the need for the story to be told fully. As I try to convey what emerges from the documents and other sources is not a story of heroes and villains, as much as it a case of a political struggle with significant issues at stake which was marked by idealism, opportunism, unintended consequences and misjudgment.

After that event, the story moves to the 1961-1982 period–the "maturing university" as William T. Jerome described the institution of which he became president in 1963. The fourth chapter focuses on the Jerome (1963-1970) and Hollis Moore (1970-81) presidencies, marked during the 1960s by expansion on the foundations started by McDonald albeit with Jerome's flair and during the 1970s by accommodation to financial constraints.

For the period since 1982, I have devoted a chapter each to the presidencies of Paul Olscamp and Sidney Ribeau, and the Conclusion takes a look at the start of the presidency of Carol A. Cartwright. The extended treatment of the Olscamp and Ribeau presidencies is to report on the "transformative leaders" who sought to reorient the University's focus.

This project traces the University history largely through the leadership of its 10 presidents. Presidents continue to set the tone and direction of the University. I benefited from the advice and support of many persons. President Ribeau provided funding for released time and a graduate assistant in 2006-07 and President Carol Cartwright, along with Simon Morgan-Russell, dean of the College of Arts and Sciences, funded a fall semester 2009 post-retirement appointment that facilitated completion of the book. Jennifer Ricker was an industrious and resourceful assistant.

I have tried to focus on significant developments, but that is not to say that everything or everyone of significance is mentioned.

The previously mentioned University History Advisory Committee–comprised of Clif Boutelle, Dick Edwards, Dana Nemeth and Terry Rentner–was indispensible, offering thoughtful and well-considered counsel on a number of matters.

The staff of the Center for Archival Collections, which houses the records of the University, was enormously helpful: Steve Charter, Head/University Archivist; Dana Nemeth, Library Associate II; Bob Graham, Archivist, Historical Collections of the Great Lakes; Lee McLaird, Curator of Rare Books; Marilyn Levinson, Curator of Manuscripts; Eric Honneffer, Conservator; Ann Jenks, former Head/University Archivist. Among the records at the CAC the oral histories conducted on the occasion of the 75th anniversary provide rich insight into the period from World War II to the early 1980s. I used the transcripts of the oral histories of Iris Andrews, Charles Barrell, Bruce Bellard, Ashel Bryan, Joseph Buford, Sam Cooper, Don Cunningham, John and Ruth Davidson, Richard Eakin, Michael Ferrari, Lyle Fletcher, Pat Gangwer, Carl Hall, Heinlen Hall, George Howick, William T. Jerome, Paul Jones, Robert

Keefe, J. Paul Kennedy, Edward Morgan, Marian Moore, Paul Olscamp, Doyt Perry, Virginia Platt, John Raney, Amy Torgerson, Duane Tucker, Robert Twyman, Raymond Yeager, Karl Vogt and Charles Young. These histories helped in bringing the "human dimension" to the University's past.

In addition, I conducted informal interviews (and in some cases follow-up questions) with a number of persons familiar with more recent developments at the University. These include: George Agich, Sue Arpad, David Bryan, Ramona Cormier, Carol Cartwright, Jill Carr, Sue Crawford, Chris Dalton, Ed Danziger, Albert Dyckes, John Folkins, Mark Gromko, John Hoag, Milt Hakel, Lou Katzner, Mike Marsh, Larry Miles, Dick Newlove, Don Nieman, Doug Smith and Jim Tucker. My notes on these conversations are being given to the CAC.

A number of other colleagues answered requests for information: Bob Bortel, Jim Foust, Matt Fredericks, Jeff Grilliot, Bill Knight, Marcia Sloan Latta, Jan Varney-McKnight, Dave Moody and Carney Strange. I am also indebted to Thelma Riehle for sharing her research on the off-campus centers and to John Schumm

for assistance in gaining recollections of former students, including Ben and Katharine Schnieder, Doug Johnson and Mildred Peoples Ringer. Special thanks to Dick Edwards and Jim Gordon, who provided personal books, papers and other sources that were very helpful. The Centennial Commission, chaired by Larry Weiss and Kim McBroom, gave its support to the suggestion that the 100th anniversary history should be more than a monograph, with more photographs than the earlier histories and the inclusion of sidebar stories, many provided by guest authors. Kim McBroom as chief communications officer and Julie Carle as communications manager have been enthusiastic in their support of this project. Julie Carle was responsible for the production phase.

Lastly, in working on this project, I have been repeatedly reminded that it is a history, not an encyclopedia. I have tried to focus on significant developments, but that is not to say that everything or everyone of significance is mentioned. I hope that what does emerge is the central story of a changing institution and its accomplishments, which underline the "legacy of excellence."

› *Gary R. Hess, December 2009*

BGSU *Presidents*

Homer B. Williams, 1912-37 (Acting, January-April 1939)

Roy E. Offenhauer, 1937-38

Frank J. Prout, 1939-51

Ralph W. McDonald, 1951-61

Ralph G. Harshman, 1961-63

William T. Jerome, 1963-70

Hollis A. Moore, 1970-81

Michael R. Ferrari, Interim, 1981-82

Paul J. Olscamp, 1982-95

Sidney A. Ribeau, 1995-2008

Carol A. Cartwright, 2008-

Normal College to University

It could easily have been Van Wert State University. The Lowry Normal School Bill, enacted by the Ohio General Assembly and signed by Governor Judson Harmon on May 19, 1910, provided for the establishment of normal schools in northeastern and northwestern Ohio, but it left the location of those institutions to an independent commission.

Ohio Gov. Judson Harmon signed the legislation to establish normal schools in northwestern and northeastern Ohio.

In northwest Ohio, 17 towns and cities[1] sought to be home of the normal school. The field was finally narrowed to Bowling Green and Van Wert, and the commission in November 1910 voted 3 to 2 in favor of Bowling Green. In the decisive vote, one member voted twice for Bowling Green, casting his own vote as well as the proxy of another member who was absent.

The Lowry Act reflected the transformation of teacher training in Ohio. At the turn of the 20th century, Ohio was one of only six states that did not provide for state-funded normal school training. This was ironic in that as early as 1836 the Ohio legislature had commissioned a study of the early European state-supported normal schools. The ensuing report strongly recommended that a comparable system be established. Although that report influenced the decision of several states to fund teacher training schools, authorities in Ohio ignored its recommendation. This had left teacher training to numerous private normal schools and academies and short-term training institutes. As the population of Ohio expanded, the deficiencies of the reliance on private efforts, both in the quality and quantity of their products, became increasingly evident. An 1899 report lamented

that "fully one-fourth [of Ohio's teachers] pass into the schoolroom as new untried instructors each year. One winter the 'big boy' in the back seat of his school, the next winter the 'teacher' seeking to guide his former classmates."

In the early years of the 20th century, this deplorable situation prompted a movement among civic groups and the State Board of Education to provide for state-funded teacher training. The private schools strongly opposed such reform claiming that Ohio did not need more colleges, so that when the Ohio legislature in 1902 took the first step toward state-funded teacher training, it did so by providing for state-supported normal schools in association with two long-established institutions: Ohio University and Miami University. Five years later, the legislature provided for teacher training at Ohio State University.

Soon the State Board of Education and members of the legislature from northern Ohio mounted a campaign for additional state-supported normal schools to meet the needs of an industrialization-spurred growing population. They had to overcome, however, the formidable opposition of private schools, which for several years blunted normal school bills. Gradually that resistance was overcome, as more civic groups in northern Ohio became actively involved in lobbying for normal schools. In those endeavors, Bowling Green, with a number of its leading citizens including State Senator R.A. Beattie in

---

1   Besides Bowling Green, Van Wert, Findlay, Fremont and Napoleon, the other cities and towns which applied for the northwest Ohio school were: Carey, Columbus Grove, Delphos, Fostoria, Grand Rapids, Kenton, Leipzig, Lima, Perrysburg, Sandusky, Upper Sandusky and Wauseon.

the vanguard, was among the most energetic communities. In 1908, Beattie introduced a bill providing for the establishment of a normal school at Bowling Green, but it was just one of 17 bills for normal schools introduced that year, none of which were ever voted on. So by 1909 a coordinated campaign of civic groups and legislators from both northeastern and northwestern Ohio emerged. Working closely with state education officials, they crafted legislation, which sought to gain support of representatives of rural counties throughout the state by adding a provision for the inclusion of training in agriculture. In January 1910, Representative John Hamilton Lowry of Henry County, a farmer and former schoolteacher who had long championed the expansion of education, sponsored the Normal School Bill. The coordinated campaign and broadened definition of teacher training paid off, as both houses of the legislature passed the Lowry Bill by substantial margins.

Now the scramble over the location of the schools began. To promote objectivity, the membership of the governor-appointed commission to determine the locations was drawn from central and southern parts of the state; it included two academics, a retired banker, a newspaperman and retired businessman. In reviewing applications from prospective homes of the new schools, the committee was to consider several factors, including: (1) a central location within the region; (2) population within a 25-mile radius; (3) availability of railroad facilities; (4) moral atmosphere, and (5) availability of suitable land for the school. Among the communities seeking the northwest Ohio school, Findlay was ineligible since the Lowry Act precluded locating the school in cities with existing colleges. This proved helpful to Bowling Green in that civic leaders in both Findlay and Toledo, which as the home of Toledo University was also ineligible, supported Bowling Green's candidacy.

Three other cities, however, provided attractive proposals to the commission. Offering a beautiful site along the Maumee River, Napoleon appeared at one point to be the front-runner, but its application was rejected, because "numerous saloons" raised questions about the community's "moral atmosphere." That left Fremont, Van Wert and Bowling Green as the prime contenders.

Fremont's bid emphasized the attractiveness of locating the school at Spiegel Grove, including 84 acres of land and the Rutherford B. Hayes Memorial Library. The cost of acquiring that proposed site and adjoining property appeared to be prohibitive, and the state was unwilling to assume responsibility for the Hayes Library, thus ending Fremont's prospects. In the end, the choice came down to Bowling Green and Van Wert. On Thursday, Nov. 10, 1910, the commission—in that narrow vote—selected Bowling Green. (Shortly afterward, Kent was selected as the site of the northeastern Ohio school.)

A number of factors worked in Bowling Green's favor. Civic leaders in nearby Findlay, Toledo, and (after elimination) Fremont and Napoleon, supported Bowling Green's bid. They preferred Bowling Green to the distant Van Wert. In addition, the breadth and commitment of the Bowling Green community leadership impressed the commission. Most importantly, Bowling Green better met three important selection criteria: central location within the northwest district, accessibility to railroads and availability of a large tract of land.

The city of Bowling Green offered four possible locations, including an 82.5-acre tract of land on the east side of town that included the city park. According to legend, when the commission visited the prospective sites in Bowling Green, one member stood in the park with its grove of trees and proclaimed, "this, gentlemen is where the new normal school should be located!" In the end, his fellow commissioners agreed. Reporting on the decision, the *Cleveland Plain Dealer* proclaimed, "At Bowling Green the state will receive a magnificent natural park inside the limits of the city where the school will be located."

Bowling Green, the seat of Wood County, was a small residential community with a population of about 6,000. The city dates its origins to 1833, but in the early years few people were attracted to the region because much of it was a marshland commonly known as the Black Swamp. In the mid-19th century, the construction of an extensive irrigation system transformed the swamp into a rich farming area. With the discovery of oil and natural gas in 1886, Bowling Green and other small towns experienced a boom, which included a number of

Representative John Lowry of Henry County sponsored the Normal School Bill, which set the stage for expanding educational opportunities in northwest Ohio.

Bowling Green offered the right atmosphere to locate the new normal school; the first commencement was held at the Chidester Theatre.

glass factories. By the time that Bowling Green became the home of the new normal school, the boom had ended. Bowling Green resumed its earlier character as a community in the midst of rich farmland, the home to several small businesses and the county government.

Launching the new school took longer than anticipated. Classes were not offered until 1914, and then in makeshift off-campus facilities. The delay resulted from unexpected obstacles in converting the site of the school into a functioning campus. To take full possession of the tract of land, the City of Bowling Green had to gain public support of a $50,000 bond issue, which was approved by voters in January 1911 by an overwhelming 947 to 11 vote. A small group of citizens, who opposed the normal school, then challenged the legality of the city's plan to donate the park to the state. When city officials discovered

that Ohio law prohibited the direct transfer of property to the state, they decided to auction the park with the expectation that it would be purchased by a citizen who supported the school and who, in turn, would give it to the state. There were fears that opponents would enter the bidding. The auction, however, went according to the city's script. In October 1911 a large group of citizens gathered in the park where it was auctioned (for the sum of 10 dollars) to a representative of the city, who in turn transferred title to the state (for 1 dollar). That did not end problems, as land titles to adjoining properties were defective. Adjudication took several months and the process was further delayed when some landholders demanded greater compensation than the city was offering. Thus it was only after considerable negotiation and legal maneuvering that title to the 82.5 acres was transferred to the state.

By that time the General Assembly had authorized $150,000 for the construction of buildings, with the understanding that future construction costs would be limited to an additional $100,000. The $250,000 commitment (about $3.65 million in 2010 dollars) was half of the $500,000 building construction budget that officials in Columbus had promised both of the new schools when the Lowry Act had been passed. Thus, the very first appropriation from the state marked the beginning of a long history of disappointing support from Columbus. Harsh winter weather further delayed the building program, meaning that it was not until early 1913 that the first groundbreaking took place. By contrast, Kent State Normal School began off-campus extension courses in 1912 and offered its first on-campus courses in May 1913.

Other aspects of planning for the institution moved along well, reflecting the vision of the five-member Board of Trustees that the Governor appointed in 1911. Comprised of two businessmen, a teacher-turned farmer, a banker and an educator—all from northwest Ohio—the board immediately began the search for a president. After interviewing two candidates, the board settled on Homer B. Williams, who had been superintendent of schools in Sandusky since 1898. Highly respected among educators in the state, he was at the time of his appointment the president of the Ohio State Teachers Association. The Board offered the position to the 46-year-old Williams in February 1912 and three months later, he began what proved to be a long tenure as president. Williams, who held a bachelor's degree from Ohio Northern University and a master's degree from Baldwin-Wallace College, had taught in several rural schools before moving into administration. He had served as superintendent at four schools prior to going to Sandusky.

At the meeting where Williams' appointment was announced, the board also gave the institution its name: Bowling Green State Normal College. The name "normal college" was of significance, for it indicated that the Board of Trustees, in consultation with Williams, envisioned an institution that would be more than the "normal school" authorized by the Lowry Act. This designation reflected a movement in teacher training away from the traditional two-year normal school training. Recognizing the need for

more secondary teachers to meet the demands of expanding high school education and the inadequacy of two-year programs for elementary teachers, a number of states had moved toward establishing four-year degree-granting programs of teacher education. The "teachers college" was thus gradually replacing the "normal school." The name "normal college" adopted by the Board of Trustees was something of an anomaly, reflecting both the passing and future modes of teacher training. It did, nonetheless, highlight that the board anticipated the offering of four-year programs. Williams and many others never liked the "normal college" name and a practice developed early of referring to "Bowling Green College," including some of the school's publications.

The "normal college," however, did immediately move beyond the "normal school." The first curriculum, crafted in 1913-14, included the traditional two-year programs, but also had three-year diploma programs—indicative of the thinking of the trustees and the president that Bowling Green would soon move toward degree programs. Williams observed, somewhat disingenuously, that nothing in the Lowry Act prohibited the granting of degrees. Kent State had already announced plans to offer the bachelor's degree in pedagogy if there was sufficient demand. In 1915, Kent State followed Bowling Green's lead when its trustees changed that institution's name to Kent State Normal College.

The new institutions' resistance to the limitations of the "normal school" designation defied the intent of the Lowry Act and the State Department of Education. Ohio State University was referred to as the only degree-granting teacher education program; the four other state schools were to offer two-year courses for training teachers. Their assertions of autonomy did not go unnoticed and were soon challenged by state officials and Ohio State University leadership.

By the time the Bowling Green curriculum was in place, Williams had recruited faculty for the new college. In September 1913 the Board of Trustees granted him a leave to study college administration at the renowned Columbia University Teachers College, where he recruited faculty and earned a master's degree with an emphasis on college administration. In identifying faculty mostly from Columbia and elsewhere in the East, Williams disappointed a number of

Homer B. Williams, superintendent of Sandusky (Ohio) schools, was selected to be the first president at Bowling Green Normal College.

'The Best Class Ever'
The First Commencement: July 29, 1915

Bowling Green's first commencement ceremony occurred less than a year from the school's opening and before any classes had been offered on campus. The graduates, who had begun their studies at a Toledo private school, entered Bowling Green State Normal College as seniors. They needed only an additional year of training to complete the two-year elementary teacher diploma. By taking courses at Bowling Green's Toledo branch, 35 women thus constituted the first graduating class– "the best class ever at BGSNC" one of them proclaimed in her scrapbook.

During the week prior to the commencement, President Williams hosted a reception in the graduates' honor and the Philharmonic gave a concert to commemorate their accomplishment. The "Feast of the Little Lanterns" highlighted, among other things, the class song with its "normal" chorus:

> Here's to the Senior class
> Of the Normal School
> The year 19 - 15
> We have gained much knowledge
> In our normal college
> Now we're almost Normal too.
> We have never shirked
> We have always worked
> And kept our brain all whirl.
> For real social efficiency
> Here's to the Normal Girl.

Helen Eunice Crom was the first class president; in 2010 she was posthumously named one of BGSU's 100 Most Prominent Alumni.

On the morning of Thursday, July 29, the commencement was held at the Chidester Theatre in downtown Bowling Green. The significance of the occasion was evident, as all board members and various state officials were in attendance. The Philharmonic performed and Professor Hesser sang a solo. Helen Eunice Crom, the class president, presented the class history, and Bernice A. Mayhew, class vice president, spoke on "Teacher Training in Ohio in State Supported Schools." The principal address, "The Cultivation of Initiative in Students," was delivered by Professor Charles H. Judd, the director of the school of education at the University of Chicago. Thus, the first of Bowling Green's commencements reflected dignity and spirit that has characterized nearly all subsequent graduations.

northwest Ohio candidates for teaching positions, most of whom had some political backing but had marginal qualifications. Williams, however, did include among his recruits two teachers with whom he had worked at Sandusky High School. Altogether, Williams recruited seven men and three women who, joined by four critic teachers for the elementary training school, comprised the first members of the faculty. While Williams' recruits generally proved to be outstanding teachers, none brought experience at the collegiate level. Comparisons with Kent State in these early years are inevitable and instructive. Its Board of Trustees selected the teacher-training supervisor (and briefly president) at Western Illinois State Normal School as its president; he in turn hired faculty with collegiate teaching experience.

Facing criticism for not opening as early as Kent State, Williams made plans to begin classes in 1914. Facilities on campus would not be ready for another year. Construction, which moved slowly, started with the Administration Building (later renamed University Hall). That building included classrooms, auditorium, gymnasium and offices. It was part of a planned cluster of buildings to be located at the east end of an extended Court Street. A science building, elementary training school and women's dormitory as well as a heating plant (located behind what is now University Hall) comprised the original campus.

While the construction on those buildings progressed, Bowling Green State Normal College finally opened in September 1914. The faculty maintained a hectic teaching schedule that took them from classes in Bowling Green to Toledo and other communities. The faculty included: George Wilson Beattie, agriculture; Mary Turner Chapin, home economics; Ernest G. Hesser, music; Dallas D. Johnson, education; Josephine Forsythe Leach, supervisor of practice teaching and director of the Toledo branch; Rea McCain, English; Edwin L. Moseley, biology; James Robert Overman, mathematics; Ernest G. Walker, extension; Leon Loyal Winslow, industrial arts.

Most classes were held in the Armory at the corner of East Wooster Street and Prospect Street, with the library housed diagonally across the street in the basement of the Methodist Church; the church was also the site of weekly chapel classes. The elementary training school was in the

Some of the classes during the first year were held in the Bowling Green Armory.

nearby original Ridge Street School. In addition, second-year classes were taught in Toledo to accommodate students in a now-defunct private teacher-training school. Faculty normally taught six days a week, three in Bowling Green and three in Toledo, which was reached by the interurban trolley line. In addition to these diploma-oriented courses, the College also met the needs of teachers throughout northwestern Ohio who needed additional training to meet additional professional requirements. Extension courses for in-service teachers were offered in 24 centers, in addition to a substantial six-week summer term. Nearly 80 percent of Bowling Green's first students were enrolled in the extension and summer programs. Indeed enrollment during 1914-15 provided abundant evidence that the fledgling school was meeting a definite need: 304 students were in the academic year programs, 598 in the extension program and 615 in the summer school. This pattern of enrollment in extension and summer classes exceeding that of the regular academic year continued for the next several years.

The young women who had begun the two-year teacher training in the private program in Toledo came to Bowling Green State Normal College as "seniors" needing one year of

instruction to earn their diplomas. In their "class history," they used a nautical metaphor to describe the new school as having saved them after the demise of the Toledo school:

" *We are in danger of shipwreck … but we are sighted in the distance by a ship, which immediately hastens to rescue us. As it approaches, we can distinguish a large brown and orange flag upon which are the letters BGNC. … We meet the captain Miss Leach and learn the other officers: Mr. Johnson, chief officer on the normal curve … Mr. Overman, our mathematician, Miss McCain, who guides the crew in matters of correct speech, our naturalist from Sandusky Prof. Moseley … the director of the orchestra Mr. Hesser … our artist Mr. Winslow: 'It's really a shame girls, you don't have a course with Mr. Winslow' … then appeared the humorist who loves Indiana and banks, Mr. Walker and the man who is interested in poultry Mr. Beattie, and last but not the least our chief cook, Miss Chapin. In the background looms the form of our new chief engineer, Dr. Williams. Smooth seas, sailing is excellent. The work is arranged and we begin our practice teaching and have delightful conferences with Miss Leach. Not only our work, but also our vocabularies are changing. We now hear such words as problem, motivation, efficiency, curves and one man persists in greeting us with new concepts, saying, 'I want to get your reaction to this.'* "

The next academic year, 1915-16, found the College functioning fully on campus, with the opening of the North Dormitory (the first building to be completed and soon christened by students as Williams Hall, which the Board of Trustees formally designated in 1917), University Hall and (by the spring semester) the Science Building (later named Moseley Hall). Also, a remodeled house facing East Wooster Street became the home of the president.

Construction also began on the Elementary School Building (later Hanna Hall), which was to be ready by 1917. The shortage of materials caused by World War I and the bankruptcy of the original contractor delayed the construction; it stood half-built for several years—not until 1921 was it finished, thus completing the original campus. Also, the plan for a traffic circle in front of University Hall was realized when the City of Bowling Green vacated the portion of Court Street on campus and of Wayne Street, a north-south street running from East Wooster to Ridge Street. By the time faculty and students were occupying the campus in the fall of 1915, the College had committed itself to offering four-year degree courses for high school teachers and supervisors. The first degree—the Bachelor of Science in education—was awarded in 1917, and there were eight more in 1918. So within four years of its opening, Bowling Green State Normal College had moved on its own initiative to become a degree-granting institution. Most students, however, continued to work toward the two-year diplomas. During the first six years, Bowling Green typically awarded between 50 and 60 diplomas annually, mostly in elementary education with a few in home economics, music and industrial arts.

Knowledge of subject matter was a high priority to President Williams and the faculty.

Bowling Green's "holding power" (what later would be called "retention") was of concern from the beginning. At the time the generally accepted standard was that 75 percent of first-year students would return for the second year. During its first decade, Bowling Green never approached that level, with only about one-third of freshmen returning as sophomores. Not until 1924-25 did the retention rate go above 50 percent. Combined with the fact that the vast majority of students were in two-year programs, this "holding power" problem meant that a majority of students were freshmen, typically accounting for 60-70 percent of the student body until the mid-1920s. Even with more students enrolling in four-year programs by the late 1920s, freshmen still constituted at least 50 percent of the student body.

Knowledge of subject matter was a high priority to President Williams and the faculty. While the diplomas/degrees offered were only in education, liberal arts fields were a significant part of the curriculum. One by-product of that emphasis was that a number of students who were interested in earning undergraduate degrees in arts and sciences would study for a year or two at Bowling Green and then transfer to a four-year liberal arts college; because most such students were young men, the liberal arts offerings increased the number of male students. Also, the Bowling Green degree programs in education attracted mostly men. This meant that by the late 1920s, as enrollment approached 1,000 students, men comprised about one-fourth of the student body.

As the faculty and offerings expanded over the next few years, the catalogues listed offerings in 14 departments (although some offered few courses and had just one faculty member). Integral to the vision of serving the needs of the citizens of northwest Ohio was the determination of the board, president and faculty to keep the cost of education at an affordable level. Until 1920, the financial needs for operations and construction of buildings were met entirely by state appropriations. No tuition was charged. Students living on campus (available only to women until 1939) paid $76.50 for room and board. Together with the cost of books and supplies, it was estimated that total expenses per year were about $200.

Inevitably, costs increased. Room and board increased modestly during the 1920s, reaching $90 per semester. At the same time, in what was to become a chronic feature of state support of higher education, officials in Columbus said in 1916 that the state had reached its limit in terms of funding the five state-supported institutions. They would need to determine new means of income. This meant passing more of the costs to students. Bowling Green imposed a modest $2 per semester activity fee, but in 1920 was obliged to add a registration fee, a euphemism for tuition, of $10 per semester. With that fee increasing to $22.50 in 1926, the estimated total cost of a year's schooling for on-campus students was $280 by the end of the 1920s, or a 40 percent increase during that decade. Still what stands out in Bowling Green's financial picture in the late 1920s is that the state appropriations were covering 80-90 percent of operating expenses.

During the early years, a number of student activities, some of which proved enduring, were established. These groups all faced the challenge of providing continuity in what was a very transitory student body. It was estimated that about 60 percent of students voluntarily joined in some extra-curricular activity.

The first student group was Book and Motor, which recognized scholastic achievement. Inspired

The Builders: The Early Faculty

Critical to Bowling Green's early sense of purpose and accomplishment was the quality of the faculty, mostly recruited by President Williams. The initial faculty hired for the opening 1914-15 academic year and those hired over the next several years shaped the institution. Of special significance were six men and women who began as the sole instructor in his or her discipline and shaped the departments and the University during careers that stretched from 18 to 45 years: Edward Lincoln Moseley, James Robert Overman, Rea McCain—three of Williams' initial recruits—Laura Heston, Daniel Crowley and Clayton C. Kohl—who joined the faculty during the next six years.

Edwin Lincoln Moseley was the most eccentric, but also the most renowned, of the early professors. By the time that he joined the faculty in 1914, he was an established teacher-scholar. Forty-nine years old and with bachelor's and master's degrees from the University of Michigan, he had taught science at Sandusky High School (where Williams had been superintendent) and had been the longtime secretary (and later president) of the Ohio Academy of Science. At Bowling Green, he taught all the sciences and authored three general science textbooks. Throughout his long career, he published numerous papers in different scientific fields, but he was primarily a biologist and naturalist. Moseley engaged hundreds of students in hands-on observations of nature in northwest Ohio, leading them on field trips as they hurried to keep up with his running lecture. He retired in 1936. His death in 1948 was noted in leading newspapers, including the *New York Times*. He endowed a substantial scholarship and Moseley Hall was named in his honor in 1951.

James Robert Overman, more than any faculty member in the University's history, was at the center of the University's development. Technically the first faculty member hired by Williams, Overman, a Columbia University graduate, established the mathematics department and was its sole instructor for several years. Overman was a dedicated teacher who authored textbooks on mathematics and the teaching of mathematics. He held numerous "firsts" including first chairman of the mathematics department, first librarian, first registrar, first dean of the college of liberal arts, first dean of men, first advisor of *The Key* and first dean of the faculties. He retired in 1956 after 42 years service

and four years later, upon the completion of a large addition to the Chemistry Building, the entire building was named in his honor.

Rea McCain was at the center of the development of the humanities. A graduate of National Norman University and Columbia University, McCain introduced the study of literature, poetry and public speaking in the classroom. In addition, she sponsored the student literary societies, directed the first plays on campus, coached the debate teams and organized chapters of honor societies. After retiring from Bowing Green in 1953, she headed the humanities division at Bishop College in Texas for several years.

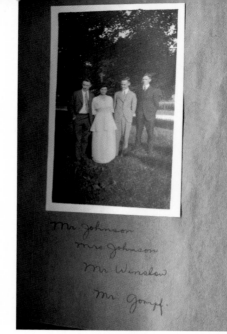

Some of the early faculty members, pictured in May Lambert's scrapbook. Courtesy of the BGSU Center for Archival Collections.

The longest serving of the early faculty was Laura Heston, who came to Bowling Green in 1919, when home economics was designated as one of five diploma-granting areas. A graduate of Ohio State University, she stayed for 45 years (35 as department chair), retiring in 1964. Under her leadership, the department grew to nearly five faculty with 100 majors per year. She recalled the early years: "Of course, it was just a small school getting started but the teachers were dedicated. There weren't many of us and we took on every job that needed to be done."

Also coming on board in 1919 and serving almost as long as Heston was Daniel Crowley in industrial arts. While building the curriculum in that field, Crowley was responsible for the development of the graphic arts program. Committed to a faculty voice in governance before it was commonly accepted, he played an instrumental role in forcing the Board of Trustees to abandon the secretive and politically charged process surrounding the appointment of Williams' successor in 1937. By the time of his retirement in 1960, there were six faculty and 120 majors in the industrial-graphic arts department.

Clayton C. Kohl, who was appointed professor of social science in 1920, had the distinction of being the first faculty member to hold an earned doctorate at the time of his appointment. Like the other "founders," he was initially a one-person department, teaching courses in economics, political science and sociology. When university status was attained, he played a prominent role in the development of the graduate program. He died unexpectedly in November 1938; the following month the first men's dormitory, which was under construction, was named in his honor—the first time that a building's name recognized a faculty member.

Kohl Hall, named after social science professor Clayton C. Kohl, today houses the Chapman Learning Community.

by the suggestion of Professor Leon Winslow who designed a gold key for the society—and with the assistance of his colleagues James Robert Overman and Rea McCain—the group was established during the school's first year when it had its first class of 35 seniors. Four of them were elected to membership. Election to Book and Motor soon became the highest honor for seniors.

The most popular and influential of the early groups was the Country Life Club, advised by agriculture professor George W. Beattie, which attracted hundreds of students to its monthly meetings. It spawned other activities; most notably it launched and supported the student newspaper, the *Bee Gee News*, which was first published on May 20, 1920. For the next decade, the *Bee Gee News* was published monthly, its pamphlet-size issues appearing 10 times a year. It became a weekly publication in 1931.

As the *Bee Gee News* took root, the publication of a yearbook proved more difficult. The first student publication was, in fact, an annual, named *The Bee Gee*, which appeared in the spring of 1918. Although that publication was an artistic and financial success, plans for annual yearbooks did not materialize, largely because the faculty supervisor, Leon Winslow, resigned from the faculty. At the initiative of the Country Life Club, the yearbook project was revived in 1924, when, with strong support from administration, faculty, students and alumni, the first *Key* yearbook was published and, unlike its predecessor, endured, becoming a fixture of student life for the next 70 years.

Literary societies—a staple of student life on campuses at that time—began as early as the 1914-15 academic year with the founding of the Wilsonian and Emersonian Literary Societies. These groups, which thrived for the next 20 years, emphasized "developing social graces, logical thinking and oral expression." Fraternities and sororities took root slowly, in part because Williams opposed the use of Greek names until the school would be eligible for chapters of national groups. Two early efforts at establishing fraternities failed after a few years. In the 1920s several local sororities—Seven Sisters, Five Sisters, Skol, Three Kay—were launched (some undergoing name changes and reorganization, in a couple instances necessitated by losing all members to graduation). At the same time, despite the small number of men students, three local fraternities—Five Brothers, Delhi and Commoners—were firmly established. These sororities and fraternities survived until the arrival of national Greek societies 20 years later.

Paralleling the development of student publications and despite the dearth of male students, Bowling Green ventured into the world of intercollegiate athletics, which at the time meant "men's sports." In 1916-17, Bowling Green fielded its first team—in basketball—which played an eight-game schedule, winning just two games. The first game was against Toledo University, which became Bowling Green's principal athletic rival. Toledo prevailed in that initial contest, 33-18. In the spring of 1918, Bowling Green added a baseball team. With few male students (just 24 in 1916-17 and 28 in 1917-18), Bowling Green's first teams included mostly novice players and lacked any depth. In the fall of 1919, Bowling Green, with a total enrollment of 36 male students, fielded its first football team, which played and lost three games. At the same time, Bowling Green joined with Bluffton College, Defiance College, Findlay College and Toledo University to form the Northwest Ohio Intercollegiate Athletic Conference. Two years later Bowling Green, thanks to a 20-7 victory over Toledo, claimed its first conference championship.

As by-product of a significant increase in male students (from a handful to 200-250 by the end of the 1920s), Bowling Green was able to restrict participation in varsity sports to sophomores and above.

The first *Bee Gee News* was published 10 times a year.

The long-standing involvement of the music program in the campus and community cultural life began early. The present Bowling Green Philharmonia traces its origins to the eight-person orchestra, including seven students and one faculty member, which was established at President Williams' request in 1918. The paucity of musicians kept the orchestra at a minimal number and was temporarily discontinued before Merrill C. McEwen revived it in 1922 by recruiting students, faculty as well as townspeople to join. The orchestra became a fixture at many occasions, including the chapel services, commencement and basketball games.

Paralleling the orchestra's revival was the organization of the first marching band in 1923. Comprised officially of "students of both sexes who play acceptably" but unofficially "of all students and faculty who can toot a horn," the band numbering 20-some men made its first appearance at the Homecoming football game that fall. (Women would not become marching band members until 1943.)

Beginning in its first year, Bowling Green commemorated the arrival of spring with a major musical event that lasted three or four days. Concerts were held in the auditorium of the Methodist Church or in a downtown theatre. For several years, a Spring Musical Festival featured the May Festival Chorus comprised of "any singer in college or in the city of Bowling Green" which performed "renditions of great choral works." Later visiting artists and orchestras, including the Minneapolis and Cleveland symphonies, appeared. The Spring Musical Festival ended in 1920 with the departure of its founder, G. W. Hesser. In 1924 a new spring celebration was started. At the initiation of a romance language instructor, the first May Fete was held. Borrowing from British custom, it was marked by a "royal procession" of the May Queen (elected by the students), members of her "court," and children from the on-campus training school participating as "heralds, jesters, train bearers, crown bearers and flower girls," which was followed by the crowning of the queen and the "winding of the beribboned Maypole."

Day-to-day campus life reflected the College's *en locus parentis* role. Women students adhered to a written code of conduct, which restricted their attire and behavior. A system of demerits penalized a wide range of infractions, from violating mandatory quiet and study hours, engaging in "rude actions" in the dining room and other public areas, failing to send male callers away at required times, and even for using the bathroom between the "retiring bell" at 9:45 p.m. and the "rising bell" at 6:30 a.m. Students and faculty were required to attend a weekly Tuesday assembly, which after "brief devotional services"

Above Left:
The May Fete included a royal procession and the traditional "winding of the beribboned Maypole."

Above Right:
The first marching band organized in 1923 and performed at Homecoming that year.

Women on campus were expected to comply with conduct and dress codes.

Establishing Traditions: Alma Mater, School Colors, Mascot and Beyond

During the early years, Bowling Green took on the distinctive features of a college. In the very first year, President Williams established a faculty-student committee to select school colors. According to an oft-told story, Leon L. Winslow, one of the faculty members, recommended orange and brown as the school colors, because he had found them a striking combination on a woman's hat that that he had observed while riding the interurban trolley from Toledo. Whether or not the story was accurate (Winslow always refused to confirm or deny it), the colors soon became those of the newly established normal college.

That same year, the first instructor of music, Ernest G. Hesser, composed an alma mater, *We Hail You, Dear Normal College*, which had to be changed years later because of the elimination of "normal" from the name of the College. The first verse of the long-forgotten original alma mater:

> *We hail you dear Normal College*
> *Ohio's great seat of knowledge,*
> *O cheer then dear brothers,*
> *Sing then dear sisters,*
> *Buckeyes from this great state, Rah! Rah!*
> *We raise high the flag of victory*
> *Your fame is the whole world o'er, Rah! Rah!*
> *So shouting defiance*
> *We have reliance*
> *Winning a great big score, Rah! Rah!*

Professor Winslow designed the school seal; it was inspired by the "vision of the new Normal College as the rising sun of a great new institution." Patterned after the State Seal of Ohio, the school's seal was divided into four parts— the mountain range, the brilliant sun, a bundle of 17 arrows representing Ohio's rank in the Union and the sheaf of wheat to symbolize the state's agricultural base. "Bowling Green State Normal College" was printed around the edge. The only part of the seal to be modified over the years accommodated institutional name changes. Soon the seal inspired its own lore. Implanted in the ground in a circle in the heart of campus (between McFall Center and Williams Hall), legend has long had it that couples who kiss while standing on it will get married, and any student who jumps on it will not graduate.

The development of the athletic program inspired additional traditions. Instrumental in these initiatives was Ivan E. "Doc" Lake, a 1923 graduate and longtime sports writer for the *Bowling Green Sentinel-Tribune*. The first Homecoming, held in conjunction with a football game, was Nov. 4, 1922 with 500 alumni in attendance. The first Homecoming queen, however, was not crowned until 1931.

Early athletic teams were known as the Normals—a name which was never considered especially inspiring and, moreover, connoted a type of institution which alumni, faculty and students believed was outdated (even though it was still officially a normal college). In 1927 Lake suggested that the nickname should be changed to Falcons. It met with instant approval. Supporters of the falcon as a symbol emphasized its inspiring attributes as a small but powerful bird noted for its fierceness, speed and courage.

By the time Bowling Green State Normal College became Bowling Green State College, most of its traditions had been established, including an appropriate new nickname for the now outdated "normals."

The first homecoming, in 1922, was inspired in part by Ivan E. "Doc" Lake, a 1923 graduate.

typically featured lectures by Williams, members of the faculty or outside speakers, and, on occasion, concerts.

Although student life seemed vibrant as measured by the number of activities, a frequent complaint was the lack of school spirit. A *Bee Gee News* editorial in 1926, for instance, lamented, "the right kind of college spirit is woefully lacking in BGNC" and chastised students for being disrespectful toward visiting speakers and musical performers at the weekly assembly programs. "There isn't any reason why a normal college," the editorial concluded, "should be inferior to other colleges in school spirit."

That comparison with "other colleges" touched upon a problem of "image"—that a normal college was inferior to four-year institutions. Throughout the 1920s, Bowling Green stressed in its catalogue and other publications that it was "A Real College." A message from President Williams emphasized that it had "the same entrance credits and standards as is required at older colleges" and that its extensive extra-curricular activities "receive special attention" and "the social needs of students are carefully looked after."

Yet the rigid restrictions and structure resembled a continuation of high school. This typified the early years of teachers' colleges, for they were, in many ways closer to a public school system than they were to liberal arts colleges and universities. Williams typified that continuity, for he administered Bowling Green State Normal College in much the same manner that he had run the Sandusky Public Schools. Nearly all of the early faculty came from public school teaching positions and were accustomed to a rigid administrative hierarchy with little faculty involvement in governance.

Enjoying support from the Board of Trustees, Williams ran a tight ship. Faculty and students generally found him to be aloof and unsociable, although they respected his efforts to enhance the stature of the institution. Mostly he took pride in his frugality. To the annoyance of many faculty (and fellow presidents at other state schools), he requested minimal appropriations from the legislature and returned unexpended funds. This contributed to Bowling Green consistently receiving the lowest legislative appropriations of the five state colleges and universities, while being

held up by legislators as a model for other schools to emulate. On campus, Williams personally handled finances, determined salaries and controlled supplies, down to such details as doling out pencils and paper clips.

Williams' leadership nonetheless was instrumental to a dramatic change in Bowling Green's status within the state system. Throughout the 1920s, private liberal arts colleges and Ohio State University opposed the launching of degree-granting programs by Bowling Green Normal College and Kent State Normal College; they argued that these new schools were exceeding the intent of the Lowry Act and lacked qualified faculty and the resources necessary for training secondary school teachers or granting degrees. The principal protagonists were Ohio State and Kent State, whose leadership aggressively

A message from President Williams emphasized that ... its extensive extra-curricular activities "receive special attention" and "the social needs of students are carefully looked after."

pushed for a liberal arts college and (at times) for university status; it sought to be regarded as the northeastern Ohio equivalent of Ohio State. As part of this struggle, a committee of three Ohio State faculty visited Bowling Green and Kent; the several days spent at Bowling Green led the committee to conclude that the quality of instruction was excellent and that high standards were being maintained, but it refused to accept the proposition that Bowling Green should be anything more than a two-year normal school. President Williams took the offensive, dispatching a three-member Bowling Green faculty team to evaluate the teacher-training program at Ohio State. The committee found poor teaching, some unqualified faculty members, and inadequate supervision of practice teaching. Williams sent the report to Ohio State whose officials, more concerned with Kent State's challenge, backed away from their objections to Bowling Green's training of secondary teachers and the granting of degrees. This marked a milestone in Ohio State's support; the Bowling Green claim to collegiate status was never again seriously challenged. Yet the episode underlined that neither the name Bowling Green Normal College nor the granting of degrees had ever been explicitly authorized.

... with the enactment of the Emmons-Hanna Bill, the newly named Bowling Green State College and Kent State College moved out of the shell of the traditional normal school.

By the end of the 1920s Bowling Green's curriculum was finally given legislative sanction. In this instance, Bowling Green benefited from Kent State's persistent campaigning for a liberal arts college. After failing several times to gain legislative authorization, its leadership launched a major effort in early 1929, lining up the support of communities throughout central and northern Ohio. Senator V. D. Emmons of Akron introduced legislation giving Kent State and Bowling Green authority to offer a liberal arts curriculum and to grant both bachelor's and master's degrees. Adding Bowling Green to the legislation was a political ploy intended to gain support of legislators from the northwestern part of the state. Though leaders at Bowling Green had not been actively promoting such legislation, President Williams quickly endorsed the proposal, as did the Board of Trustees and prominent civic leaders. Williams worked with Representative Myrna Hanna of Bowling Green (for whom Hanna Hall was subsequently named) to draft the legislation, which she introduced in the House of Representatives. In the end the Emmons-Hanna Bill sailed through both houses of the General Assembly and was signed into law by Governor Myers Y. Cooper on March 28, 1929.

In its final form, the Emmons-Hanna Act both sanctioned existing programs and authorized a broader mission for both colleges. The Bachelor of Science in education degree, which had long been offered, was given formal approval. More importantly, the trustees were "authorized to establish courses leading to Bachelor of Arts

and Bachelor of Science degrees, and to elect and appoint such additional instructors as may be necessary to carry out the provisions of this section." Also, the legislation specified that the names were changed from "Normal School" (which ignored that both had called themselves State Normal Colleges) to State College. To the annoyance of many at Kent State, dropped from the legislation were provisions for graduate programs and graduate degrees and a liberal arts college was not specifically authorized. Nonetheless, with the enactment of the Emmons-Hanna Bill, the newly named Bowling Green State College and Kent State College moved out of the shell of the traditional normal school.

Faculty in those fields welcomed the authorization for degrees in liberal arts, but other faculty feared that such a development would weaken the commitment to teacher training. Although sharing some of the latter group's concerns, Williams believed that a strong liberal arts curriculum would enhance the institution. Again, the Board of Trustees exceeded the intent of the legislation, which did not authorize colleges within the new state colleges. At the suggestion of President Williams, the board promptly divided Bowling Green State College into colleges of education and liberal arts. That step anticipated the next logical step in Bowling Green's development: university status.

Before that could be realized, Bowling Green in 1933 faced a serious threat to its very existence. The Great Depression devastated the economy of Ohio, leading to drastic reductions in state revenues and to cutbacks in appropriations to state institutions. The State Senate Finance Committee proposed that one of the state colleges suspend operations to be converted, at least temporarily, into a mental hospital. As the smallest of the state colleges, Bowling Green was targeted for suspension. Within the legislature, the proposal attracted considerable support, as advocates contended that the Bowling Green students could be absorbed by the other state and private colleges, all of which were suffering economically and could benefit from more students. Not surprisingly, friends of those institutions supported the proposal. Within northwest Ohio, however, the opposition to the proposal was strong, and President Williams calculated that it would be best for citizens to take the leadership on the issue. The hastily

The Changing Campus Scene

The original set of buildings—what became known as University Hall, Williams Hall, Moseley Hall and Hanna Hall—were at last completed with the long-delayed opening of Hanna Hall in 1921. The campus also included the president's home and the heating plant. As early as 1918, Williams and the Board of Trustees anticipated the need for additional buildings and commissioned a plan for 11 new buildings, Only four were constructed in the next 20 years, but they constituted the most pressing needs.

Of highest priority was a second women's dormitory. Originally this was to be the South Dormitory, located on the other side of Court Street from the North Dormitory (now Williams Hall). Instead, the new and larger dormitory was constructed directly west of Williams Hall. Completed in 1927, it was named in recognition of the contributions of J. E. Shatzel, a North Baltimore newspaper publisher who had been prominent in Bowling Green's campaign for the normal school location and had served on the Board of Trustees from 1914-24.

Occupying the space originally intended for the South Dormitory was the Library (now McFall Center), which also opened in 1927. This first makeshift library in the Methodist Church basement had been moved to almost equally close quarters on the third floor of University Hall. At a cost of $345,000 to build and furnish, the Library had the capacity of 60,000 volumes. Its most distinctive feature was the large reference and reading room on the second floor (home of the present Faculty Senate chambers and adjacent Gallery), which seated nearly 300 persons and had wall stacks with a capacity of 6,000 volumes. Forty years later the University would outgrow the 1927 library and move to a still larger facility.

The Men's Physical Education Building (now Eppler South) became the third building to open in 1927, but was only partially completed. This was a rare instance of the normally frugal Williams lacking the funds to complete a project. The gymnasium, which became the home of the basketball team, and other facilities for physical education classes were completed, but classrooms and offices were not constructed. Williams made certain that visiting legislators would always see the half-finished building, and several years later, he had sufficient funds to complete the project.

Lastly, the Practical Arts Building (Hayes Hall) opened in 1931. The tower on top of the building was intended to house

Space was usually at a premium for the study tables in the University library, which now is McFall Center.

a set of chimes that President Williams thought would be a particularly appropriate addition to the campus. Scarcity of funds, however, precluded the purchase of chimes with the result that they were never added; for many years the tower was known as the "chicken coop" or "pigeon loft." In 1959, the building was renamed in honor of U.S. President Rutherford B. Hayes and his wife Lucy Webb Hayes, whose home was in Fremont.

Also during this era, the campus was spruced up with the construction of cement walks (replacing some hastily constructed board walks) and the addition of lights and landscaping. Framing the campus were ornamental brick and stone gateways located at the main entrances on Wooster, Thurstin and Ridge Streets. These remained distinctive landmarks until a major renovation program in the late 1950s transformed the old campus.

organized Northwest Ohio Educational Protective Association, comprised of community leaders throughout the region, worked closely but quietly with Williams to save Bowling Green State College. No one could deny the financial benefit to the state of conversion to a mental hospital, but by the same token, forcing Bowling Green students to attend other schools would increase their educational costs, including residential fees for those who commuted. Closing the College would deprive future high school graduates in northwest Ohio of an inexpensive way of attaining a college education; rather than going to school they would join the ranks of the unemployed.

Pamphlets to save Bowling Green State College were widely distributed, while faculty and civic leaders visited towns and villages, speaking to various groups and influential local citizens.

State senators and representatives were targeted for an extensive letter-writing campaign. When a subcommittee of the House Finance Committee "inspected" Bowling Green during a visit in May 1933, it was deluged by testimony opposing the school's closure from alumni, community leaders, faculty and students. The lobbying worked. In a key committee vote, a motion to delete the Bowling Green appropriation failed, 5 to 14. The proposal never resurfaced. Reporting on the outcome, the *Bee Gee News* proclaimed that "Bowling Green Is Stronger Than Ever." The grass-roots campaign to save Bowling Green State College underscored northwest Ohio residents' reliance on the College's educational leadership. Bowling Green may have had the lowest enrollment of any state college, but its enrollment withstood the Depression better than most institutions, which experienced declines

By the 25th anniversary of its founding, Bowling Green was authorized University status.

from 10-40 percent. Enrollment went above the 1,000 level for the first time in the 1930-31 spring semester and remained at that level for the next two academic years, before declining by about 10 percent in 1933-34. A notable improvement in "holding power" meant that first-to-second year retention reached 75 percent during that period. The substantial leveling of enrollment despite the Depression was best explained by the predominance of women students, the school's relatively low expenses (students tend to stay in college during periods of high unemployment if they can afford it), and the continuing demand for elementary and secondary school teachers.

The student body remained predominantly in the two-year diploma program, with three-fourths of the graduates between 1930-1935 recipients of diplomas. The growth of the degree programs—B.S.

in education, Bachelor of Science and Bachelor of Arts—resulted in more upperclassmen (about 20 percent of total enrollment). The addition of a liberal arts college and degrees did not change Bowling Green's distinctive character as a teacher-training institution. From 1930-36, graduates with a B.S. in education outnumbered the B.A. and B.S. graduates by nearly 10 times: 506 to 56.

Even at the low point of the Depression, new needs were becoming evident, notably for training in business at the undergraduate level and the offering of the master's degree, which was becoming increasingly an expectation for secondary school teachers. These pressures coincided with a growing movement in the legislature to put Bowling Green and Kent State on the same level as Ohio University and Miami University. Governor Martin L. Davey, a resident of Kent, urged the enactment of two bills by the General Assembly in 1935. These provided for renaming Bowling Green and Kent as universities, and authorizing both to establish colleges of liberal arts and business administration, and programs leading to the master of arts degree. With strong support from both political parties, Bowling Green State College became Bowling Green State University.

So within 21 years of opening, Bowling Green Normal College had attained university status. Its progress reflected the vision and opportunism of Williams and the Board of Trustees. On a political level, the persistent linking of the development of the state colleges at Kent and Bowling Green gave considerable clout in the legislature. They benefited from being able to press for the same status and support as the older schools. In some respects, university status was premature and, at best, it would require considerable curricular and administrative changes before the trappings of a university were firmly established. Still, for a state, which had been slow to embrace state-supported teacher training, the movement of Bowling Green and Kent State to university status was unique in the 1930s, as most state teachers colleges did not broaden their mission and move to universities until 30 years later. ■

1935-1960

Mission Deferred and Attained

Bowling Green's second quarter century was strongly influenced by monumental events that transformed American life. The attainment of university status in 1935 came as the nation was still in the depths of the Great Depression, but within five years the movement toward a wartime economy spurred recovery.

The Japanese attack on Pearl Harbor on December 7, 1941 plunged the United States into a war in Europe and the Pacific that lasted nearly four years. World War II changed higher education as young men went into the armed services, and colleges and universities, like other institutions in American society, were called upon in various ways to help in the fight against the Axis Powers. With the end of the war in 1945 came the challenge of adjusting to the influx of veterans, and enrollments in colleges and universities doubled almost overnight. This presented enormous staffing and housing problems. Not until the early 1950s did enrollments stabilize allowing institutions to return to a more systematic building of faculty, programs and facilities and to plan for another surge when "baby boomers" reached college age in the mid-1960s.

Thus during the period from 1935-50, the challenge of becoming a university in practice, as well as in name, had to be deferred. The

University adapted well to those momentous times, as its enrollments increased. It became less of a "teacher's college," less of a "women's college" and less of a "northwest Ohio" college. The post-war student boom transformed the University in ways that endured. The increase of male students and the development of the liberal arts and business colleges were a prelude to the strengthening of academic programs during the 1950s and the milestone reached in 1960: the start of the first Ph.D. program.

This quarter-century marked changes in leadership and the faculty's assertion of a stronger role in university governance. Early in this period, the faculty challenged the Board of Trustees' tentative choice to succeed President Homer Williams and at its end, faculty and student discontent forced the resignation of the University's fourth president in 1961. While Williams had been president for the entire first quarter-century, four presidents held office between 1935-61. Williams' service continued until 1937, when he was forced into retirement and was replaced, after a contentious selection, by Roy Offenhauer, whose untimely death after only 16 months in office, led to Williams briefly returning as acting president until a successor was appointed in April 1939. Frank J. Prout led the University through the following tumultuous decade. Upon his retirement in 1951, the Board of Trustees, with considerable faculty input, appointed Ralph W. McDonald as the University's fourth president. McDonald's presidency, which was marked by notable success in strengthening the University, ended in shambles in the most serious internal crisis of the University's history.

The distance that Bowling Green had to go before becoming a university in practice as well as in name was underscored by the predominance of teacher training and the limited number of students in liberal arts and business administration. Of the nearly 1,000 bachelor's degrees awarded between 1935-36 and 1939-40, 82 percent were in education. Adding to the predominance of education students, the State Department of Education in 1938 increased the elementary certification curriculum (as well as that in the smaller programs in music, home economics, industrial arts, commercial arts and physical education) to four-years, thus ending the two-year programs; the University awarded its last two-year diplomas in 1939.

The imbalance within the University led to a haphazard administrative structure as the Colleges of Education, Liberal Arts and the newly established Business Administration were organized. Most departments were considered liberal arts disciplines and logically belonged in that college, but only four were clearly identifiable as part of education and just one as part of business administration. Adding to the confusion, that department was named "business administration" (an economics department was added in 1936 and business education in 1940). Instead of establishing traditional colleges based on academic disciplines, the departments were divided for administrative purposes among the three deans. This meant that half of traditional liberal arts departments were responsible to either the dean of the College of Education (as were biology, history and political science and psychology) or the dean of the College of Business Administration (as were geography and geology

and sociology). Only the departments of English, foreign language, mathematics, music and physical science reported to the dean of Liberal Arts. The dean of Education also handled the departments of education, home economics and industrial arts, but physical education was assigned to the College of Business Administration. This arrangement, while parsing administrative responsibilities among three deans, stymied the development of the colleges as cohesive academic units.

While Williams earned respect for his willingness to fight for Bowling Green's interests ... some faculty and board members saw his fiscal conservatism limiting the University's growth.

The disparity between university in name and practice also characterized the manner in which the Board of Trustees dealt with the presidential transitions of 1937-40. The five-member board was comprised entirely of men from northwest Ohio and almost always included the superintendent of a public school system. This reflected the close connection between teachers colleges, public schools and state education officials and the commonly held belief that experience in administering public schools was an important qualification for leadership in teachers colleges. Although the Board of Trustees had worked for university status, its members as did residents of the region, still looked to Bowling Green as a teachers college. In many ways, the pursuit of university status was more a matter of regional pride and political opportunism than academic vision. So when the opportunity came to select new leaders, the Board of Trustees looked inward as it had 25 years earlier: to the region, to public school administrators and its recent membership.

The Board of Trustees mishandled the first presidential transition. As Williams approached the mandatory retirement age of 70 in 1936, he requested that the board allow him to continue as president, which it authorized. A year later in July 1937, however, the board, without informing Williams in advance, passed a resolution

Roy Offenhauer's presidency was cut short by his tragic death 16 months after he took office.

establishing a policy of retirement at age 70 for all employees. The vote was three-to-two and reflected a division over whether Williams, who was embittered by the board's action, had outlived his usefulness. While Williams earned respect for his willingness to fight for Bowling Green's interests in Columbus and for his political acumen, some faculty and board members saw his fiscal conservatism limiting the University's growth.

Moving hastily to appoint a successor to Williams, the Board of Trustees made no effort to conduct a "search" for the best-qualified candidate. Instead, it acted secretly and hastily in ways that undermined its credibility. It became known on campus that the board was holding secret meetings and that it was about to make an appointment based on one candidate's political connections. Students and faculty took action. Two uninvited graduate students showed up at one of the board's public meetings to state their concerns about the selection process, and a group of concerned faculty sent a two-man delegation to meet with one member of the board who was known to be the decisive vote on the prospective

appointment. The selection was complicated by the fact that the board's president, Frank J. Prout, opposed the secret process and absented himself from those meetings. In any event, the faculty initiative changed the "swing vote" and the candidacy of the "political choice" failed. In a remarkably quick decision, the Board of Trustees then selected Roy E. Offenhauer, superintendent of the Lima Public Schools, as the University's second president. Offenhauer took office in September 1937.

After Offenhauer's untimely death in December 1938 from injuries suffered in an automobile accident, the Board of Trustees undertook a hasty presidential search while Williams served as acting president for four months. Once again, the board turned to a public school leader and to Prout, its former president, whose term on the board had just expired. Like Williams, Prout was superintendent of the Sandusky public schools at the time of his appointment. The fact that Prout was known to have refused to participate in the secretive deliberations over Williams' successor enhanced his credibility with faculty. Yet some faculty thought that the search process had been too restrictive. In his history of the University's first half-century, Robert James Overman criticized the board's presidential appointments of 1937 and 1939: "In neither case did the trustees make any effort to find the best man for the position."

The role that the faculty played in the presidential selection in 1937 was paralleled by its modestly increased involvement in University governance. Williams had relied on general faculty meetings as an informational and discussion forum, in which faculty were rarely invited to make recommendations; later in his administration, he came to rely for advice on an executive committee, which included the academic deans and registrar. A number of faculty committees dealing with various student activities also had been established. Offenhauer took the first step toward more direct faculty involvement by establishing a policies commission, which included the deans as well as 10 faculty members elected by their peers. Although the policies commission lasted only three years, it was important as a forerunner to the establishment of the University Senate in 1942.

The choice of Prout, who took office on April 1, 1939, generally turned out well. In contrast with Williams, Prout was very outgoing, was highly visible on campus and in the community; he enjoyed considerable popularity, known for engaging faculty, students and local leaders in informal conversations. He had a passion for raising flowers, especially roses, earning the nickname among some friends as "the mound builder." Bruce Bellard, who joined the physical education faculty in 1949, recalled, "Dr. Prout used to walk among the students and deliver flowers to the University, raised in his gardens, and he would deliver them to the house mothers at the sororities and the fraternities and the dormitories, and he knew practically every student's name."

Iris Andrews, who came to the University in 1945 and was the longtime women's swimming coach and for whom the Andrews Pool in the Student Recreation Center is named, described Prout as "an absolutely beautiful man. He knew every student on campus. He visited the Johnston Hospital … every night to see the students who were confined there. … He was never in a hurry or too busy to listen to your problems." When students needed help (whether it be financial or just a lamp for a dormitory room), Prout would inevitably come to their aid. Robert Twyman, who joined the history faculty in 1948, said, "Frank Prout was a very fine man. I liked him and he had his heart in the right place, and would do anything for students."

Prout was considered a capable administrator, but limited in his vision for the University by his experience, never venturing beyond public schools in northwest Ohio, and his love of campus kept him in Bowling Green nearly all of the time. Twyman elaborated on that aspect of Prout's presidency:

He was all student oriented and that's obviously very good. But because he was so student oriented he was not as faculty oriented, or maybe as educationally oriented as he ought to have been. Salaries were rather low, and he never really saw any great need to try to improve them in order to attract better faculty … I liked him and I think he did good things for the University, but he did not have the making of a great university president to build the great university.

Whatever his shortcomings, Prout was clearly student oriented. He sought to broaden student activities and to engage more students in the life of the University. He built on the momentum that had accompanied the change to University status. After several years of student pressure on the issue, a system of student government had been established in 1935 with the election of representatives to a Student Council. Students also participated as members of several faculty committees

Early in his presidency, Prout championed the construction of a student union. Students had long clamored for a social center, but Williams had resisted these pressures, chiefly because student unions were generally money-losing operations. Early in his presidency, Prout, however, supported allocating a balance of $10,000 in the student fees account toward a union and to issue bonds to cover the remaining costs ($16,000). The log cabin building, promptly named the Falcon's Nest, opened in 1942 on the same site as the two later student unions.

Rose K. Calienni, who arrived at Bowling Green as a freshman in 1944, recalled that "socialization consisted of visits to the Student Union which was a log cabin. … It had an area where students would meet and dance. Dances were common most week-ends and the music was from the juke box." The Union did not satisfy all social needs; she noted that "students also frequented bars. … Howards was a favorite place. … Sorority girls often went to the 'Golden Lily' west on Route 6."

Prout was also committed to building a strong Greek system and championed the efforts of members of local fraternities and sororities to bring chapters of national groups to campus. Prout, a fraternity man, firmly believed in the value of Greek organizations. Together with a number of faculty and administrators, Prout worked with students to bring national fraternities to campus. Four colonial-style "cottage dormitories" were built in 1941-42 to house women's social groups and to attract national groups. These units, each housing 30-60 women, met the long-sought objective of the four local sororities—the Five Sisters, Skol, Seven Sisters and Three Kay, all of which dated to the mid-1920s—for their own housing facilities. Thanks to the administration's support and the new facilities,

Prior to being named president in 1939, Frank Prout was a member of the Board of Trustees.

four national sororities came to campus in 1943 replacing local ones: Five Sisters became Alpha Xi Delta; Seven Sisters became Alpha Phi; Three Kay became Gamma Phi Beta, and Skol became Delta Gamma. Las Amigas, which had been founded in 1930, gained a charter from Alpha Chi Omega in 1944. In addition, national fraternities came to campus. In fact, the earliest national Greek society to establish a chapter at Bowling Green was Pi Kappa Alpha in 1942, replacing the Commoners. Other local fraternities followed suit: Delhi received an Alpha Tau Omega chapter in 1943 and two years later, the Five Brothers fraternity became a chapter of Sigma Alpha Epsilon. The coming to campus of these four sororities and three fraternities during wartime was just the beginning. Additional chapters were quickly established during the post-war boom years.

Athletics were also integral to Prout's vision of a vibrant campus. Don Cunningham, who worked in coaching and athletic administration for many years, said, "He loved sports and loved to win." He helped make Bowling Green a "winner," as he was instrumental in the emergence as a national basketball power. After 10 years in the unwieldy 17-team Ohio Athletic Conference, Bowling Green withdrew in 1942 and played as an independent for the next 12 years. That same year Bowling Green hired Harold Anderson, who had built a strong

Toledo University basketball team, as its head basketball coach. Anderson was, as Cunningham recalled, "a very personal person … [who] would go out and do an excellent job of talking to a young man and that young man's family about education and also playing a sport. … He was an excellent recruiter." Playing some of the nation's top teams, Bowling Green, under Anderson, was invited five times during the 1940s to the National Invitation Tournament, which at the time was considered more prestigious than the NCAA Tournament.

By the time that Prout's initiatives were being launched, the nation was at war. For four years, all aspects of American life were impacted as the nation's resources were devoted to the war effort. Like other schools, Bowling Green suffered a substantial drop in enrollment when millions of young men went into the military. On-campus enrollment in 1940-41 reached its highest point, 1,600, but then began a steady decline, plunging in 1943-44 to 842 – a nearly 50 percent drop from the pre-war peak. In that year, only 69 men were enrolled. This precipitous decline reduced offerings, forced reassignment of some faculty to other duties and threatened the financial structure of the University. In particular, Kohl Hall, which had been opened in 1939 as the first men's dormitory, had been constructed with funds raised by bonds; with few residents, the University faced the prospect of being unable to make payments on the bond issue.

The wartime crisis was largely alleviated by Bowling Green's selection to participate in the Navy College Training Program, commonly known as V-12. A member of the Board of Trustees, Dudley A. White, who was a naval officer assigned to Washington, D.C., during the war, played a vital role in securing Bowling Green's pursuit of the V-12 program. In 1939 the Civil Aeronautics Authority invited the University to participate in its Civilian Pilot Training Program; this was open to University students with the flight training taking place at the Findlay airport. Then in 1942, the Civilian Pilot Training Program was supplanted by a full-time program for Navy V-5 enlistees who were brought to campus for an eight-week instruction program; flight training was provided at Bricker Field (later the University Airport and now Wood County Airport), which was constructed

Frank Prout was strong on fraternities and sororities during his tenure as president.

Silver Anniversary Celebration: 1939

With more than 1,000 alumni and friends of the University in attendance, BGSU celebrated its 25th anniversary on the commencement weekend of June 3-5, 1939. It also marked a presidential transition. Frank Prout, who had assumed office on April 1, was formally welcomed as the third president and presided over University ceremonies for the first time. President emeritus Homer B. Williams and four members of the original faculty were honored: James Robert Overman, who was then dean of the College of Arts and Sciences; Rea McCain, head of the English Department; E. L. Moseley, professor emeritus of biology, and George W. Beattie, who had recently retired as the first and last professor of agriculture.

Governor John Bricker was the principal speaker at the convocation. With the world on the brink of war, Bricker said, "If this year's class of graduates has learned this lesson of the love of a democratic form of government, we will have gained much in the battle to save the finest form of government that the mind of man has yet conceived." Institutions like Bowling Green, Bricker continued, were vital to the nation's survival. Also featured were speakers representing the classes of 1915 and 1939: Martha Harvey Parquette and Kermit Long respectively. Actually, Mrs. Parquette could have spoken for both classes, having received a two-year diploma in 1915 and a B.S. in education in 1939.

The decision to use 1914, not 1910, as the founding date to mark the anniversary caused some criticism and confusion. There was no formal history to mark the silver anniversary. There was, however, the first known effort to write a history: the nine students in a graduate seminar in education in 1938 co-authored an 85-page research paper, "A History of Bowling Green State University."

› *Written with the assistance of Jennifer Ricker*

on property north of Poe Road that the Board of Trustees had recently purchased. The V-5 program continued through 1945; it involved about 1,000 participants who were housed and fed on campus and given instruction by University faculty, but they were they not enrolled in regular University programs.

The V-12 program, which began in July 1943 and continued until end of the war two years later, brought students who enrolled in regular University courses. The Navy, however, mandated that instruction take place in year-round 16-week sessions so that students could complete four semesters in 64-month tours of duty. The University temporarily changed its academic calendar to accommodate the V-12 program, enabling the enrollment of civilian and military students in the same courses. The V-12 program brought approximately 400 students to campus in 1943-44 and 240 in 1944-45.

The V-5 and V-12 programs not only compensated in part for the loss of male civilian students, they actually triggered a housing shortage on campus. Kohl Hall could not house all the naval students, so Williams Hall was temporarily converted into a men's dormitory, as was the top floor of Hanna Hall. The women displaced from Williams Hall were housed in another temporary dormitory established in the Women's Physical Education Building (Eppler North).

Aside from their uniforms, the V-12 students were indistinguishable from other male students. They participated in student activities, contributing to the vitalization of fraternities during the war years as well as playing on intercollegiate athletic teams. As Kenneth McFall wrote in his history of the University's early years, the V-12 students "were for all intents and purposes members of the regular student body with the exception that they were in uniforms and were required to attend indoctrination classes."

As recounted by Rose K. Calienni, "The men called 'V-12s' and 'V-5s' were quasi military and trained regularly. Some were assigned to the airport and had to spend so many hours in the air. I was invited by one of them for a ride in a plane!" Maxine "Mickey" (Campbell) Welker, who enrolled at the University in 1943, learned that the cadets "weren't mingling well with the women on campus" and developed, with the cooperation of the campus YWCA, a group called Campus Teen; in her freshman year, Welker recalled, "I organized 13 all-campus parties to supplement the social calendar."

Indeed the V-12 and V-5 students generally found Bowling Green to be a welcome assignment. Charles Codding, class of 1948 who came to Bowling Green as a cadet and later worked at the University for 50 years, recalled, "The military men on campus dated a lot of girls. The girls had to be in their dorms on weekends by 12:30, but the V-12s had to be in Kohl Hall by midnight, so all the kissing goodnight was in front of Kohl. I think you'll find a lot of V-12s married Bowling Green girls." Yet the fact of war—and that the young men on campus might soon be engaged in combat on distant fronts—had a sobering effect. James Paul Kennedy, who joined the music faculty in 1940, said, "We were kind of isolated. We didn't have any idea what was going to happen. The campus was not dormant, but it lacked the spirit of normal times."

As the end of the war approached, accrediting agencies and the U.S. Office of Education encouraged colleges and universities to plan for the postwar period, because of educational opportunities that would be available to veterans under the GI Bill of Rights. This law, passed unanimously by Congress and signed by President Franklin Roosevelt in 1944, sought to facilitate conversion to a peacetime economy by reducing the flow of veterans into the job market and to build a better-educated middle class. The GI Bill subsidized the higher education of veterans as well as well as provided housing and medical benefits while in college. The GI Bill was about to bring the greatest expansion of higher education in the nation's history. By 1947, half of all college and university students were veterans.

Like most schools, Bowling Green's planning underestimated the impending growth. Prout established a central committee, which predicted a 50 percent increase above the pre-war high enrollment of 1,600 students, or about 2,400 students. That projection quickly proved to be far too modest. The post-war years witnessed the most rapid growth in the University's history. With the war ending in the summer of 1945 and the demobilization of the armed forces, enrollments rose steadily each academic year, with veterans responsible for much of the increase. This bulge hit in the spring semester of the 1945-46 academic year, when the University enrolled 574 veterans and pushed enrollment above 2,500 students. By 1950 enrollment nearly doubled the central committee's projection. The percentage enrollment increase at Bowling Green surpassed that of the postwar boom at any of the other state universities in Ohio.

Total Enrollments: 1946-47 through 1950-51

(with the number of veterans in parentheses)

1946-47:	3,856	(1,813)
1947-48:	4,472	(1,865)
1948-49:	4,525	(1,656)
1949-50:	4,682	(1,270)
1950-51:	4,235	(624)

Male students, both veterans and non-veterans were attracted to Bowling Green by the diversity of its programs and by cost. It remained the least expensive of the state universities. The development of programs in liberal arts and business administration had accounted for an increase in male students during the late 1930s and a temporary parity between male and female students in 1938-39. That trend resumed in the postwar period when Bowling Green for the first time became a predominantly male school.

Veterans brought to Bowling Green and other schools mature students who were determined to take advantage of the opportunity to gain a college education. Donald Bowman, who joined Bowling Green as a physics professor in 1943, recalled the postwar years fondly:

The most fun there was teaching here was when the bulge came with boys coming back from the Army. That group was here to learn. They were serious about it. Those veterans really tore into the classroom and it was so much fun. You would go into the class and immediately you would be faced with questions. It showed that they had thought about what you were supposed to think about for that day.

A steadily increasing number of "traditional" male students, including recent high school graduates, was a remarkable and enduring aspect of the post-war enrollment. While veterans constituted most of the male students during the three immediate postwar years, as their numbers decreased, the number of male students steadily increased, accentuating the trend toward a predominantly male institution. The University went from 506 non-veteran males in 1946-47 to 1,855 by 1950-51.

'To the Height of Basketball Fame' Playing for the NIT Title, 1945

Legendary basketball coach, Harold "Andy" Anderson said that his 1962-63 team was his best, but the 1944-45 team did better in a national tournament than any Bowling Green team in any sport except for the 1984 NCAA hockey champions.

In attaining that singular accomplishment, the 1944-45 experience reflected the impact of the war, then in its final year, on all aspects of society. The 1944-45 squad went through its regular season schedule with a record of 22-2. Wartime travel restrictions limited nearly all of the games to the region and military base teams accounted for one-third of the opponents. The vagaries of military assignments also affected the time. All-American Wyndol Gray, who had played at Bowling Green in 1941-42 and now returned as a V-12 student, led the Falcons. During the season, team captain Joe Siegferth was called into active Naval duty; his last game on January 30 was designated "Joe Siegferth Night." Besides Gray, center Don Otten also achieved national recognition, being selected to play on the College All-Star Team.

Bowling Green was one of eight teams to participate in the National Invitation Tournament (NIT), which at the time was considered more prestigious than the newer NCAA Tournament. Playing at Madison Square Garden, the Falcons won their opening round game against Rensselaer Polytechnic Institute, 60-45, to advance to the semi-finals. Their opponent was St. Johns University and provided an opportunity to avenge a defeat at the hands of the Redmen when Bowling Green had first been invited to the NIT. This time, Bowling Green prevailed, 57-44. That brought Bowling Green to the finals against powerful DePaul University, which captured the NIT crown by a 71-54 score. As described in *The Key*," a great season, a wonderful season … took Bowling Green to the height of collegiate basketball fame and ended with the voted national basketball crown just slipping through the fingers of the greatest Falcon squad in Bee Gee history."

These changes transformed the University. Bowling Green was no longer a "women's college" as it traditionally had been viewed. Female enrollments also increased in the post-war period by about 100 students each year. With male enrollments growing at a much higher pace, men came to outnumber women by a significant margin; by the late 1940s, men constituted about 60-65 percent of the student body. Bowling Green was also no longer a "teachers college," but was now moving steadily toward offering more-diversified academic programs. Enrollments in the colleges of liberal arts and business administration grew at a faster rate than in education. In 1945-46, half of the students were enrolled in degree programs in education, but by 1949-50, the disparity among the three colleges had been reduced with about 40 percent in education, and 30 percent each in liberal arts and business administration. Finally, Bowling Green was no longer a "regional" school. Before World War II, most students lived on farms and small towns within 50 miles of Bowling Green. The training programs brought to campus young men from all over the country, some of whom chose to stay as they continued their education after the war, and the veterans who came under the GI Bill were from all parts

of Ohio and other states. These factors meant that by 1950, students came from 74 Ohio counties and 30 states.

The spectacular enrollment growth produced severe shortages in student housing, classroom space and qualified faculty. The post-war boom was marked by "temporary" measures to address these needs. The need for more buildings had to be deferred because of a nationwide shortage of building materials. The State Board of Control ruled in February 1946 that all state-funded building had to be delayed until conditions improved. The Board of Trustees had to buy existing buildings near campus or to construct temporary buildings. Anticipating the continued growth of the University, the board bought various parcels of land near campus as they became available; in the decade of the 1940s, the size of the campus grew from 105 to 274 acres.

Keeping pace with the relatively modest increase in female students proved almost overwhelming. Women students continued to be housed in Shatzel Hall, returned to Williams Hall and were assigned (temporarily) to Kohl Hall, while still others remained in the makeshift Eppler North facility. As part of the purchase of five acres south of campus, the University acquired a brick apartment building

New Traditions: Sicsic, Ay Ziggy Zoomba, Alma Mater, & Freddie

The postwar years brought notable additions to University traditions. A veteran was directly involved in the first two of them. In 1946, Gilbert Fox, class of 1948 who had served in the Air Force during the war, was asked to sing at a "spirit assembly." He spontaneously chose a song that he had learned in Italy from South African airmen which was a "loose translation of a Zulu war chant," thus giving the University its unofficial fight song, "Ay Ziggy Zoomba."

President Prout, who was committed to building school spirit and was enthralled by "Ay Ziggy Zoomba," invited Fox and five other male students to a secret meeting in his office on the night of Oct. 5, 1946. SICSIC was founded that night, announcing its existence by a public address system at 3 a.m. the following morning. "I came up with the name," Fox later revealed, "but I still can't tell anyone what it means." SICSIC members began their tradition of "donning gray bib overalls and full Halloween-style masks to make their appointed rounds by night" leaving "SICSIC says" signs written in black and red to spark enthusiasm for athletic events, the start of classes, final exams, Homecoming and other occasions. Composed of six members (two each from the sophomore, junior and senior classes), the membership is kept secret, except for revealing at the end of each year the names of its senior members. It is the oldest continually functioning student group on campus.

Four years later, another enduring tradition began with the first incarnation of Freddie Falcon, who made his debut at a Jan. 16, 1950 basketball game. Deb Novak, assistant dean of students, noted, "at this time, the first Freddie was just a papier-mâché head [which] was actually eaten by mice." Ten years later Freddie was joined by "Mrs. Freddie Falcon," who was actually a male cheerleader dressed in disguise. (Frieda Falcon, Freddie's sister, didn't come along until 1980.)

President Prout's solution to lack of school spirit, SICSIC, continues to this day as a secret society dedicated to infusing enthusiasm into school events.

A new alma mater—the University's third and the one that endures to the present—was introduced. President McDonald believed that the second alma mater, written in 1936 after University status had been attained, was outdated. In 1955 he announced a five-year competition for a "more stirring and appealing" alma mater, with the wining entry to be selected during the 50th anniversary celebration, In the end, the composition of Edith Ludwig Bell, class of 1951 who was a Lorain County school teacher, won the competition. It was first sung at the convocation of May 19, 1960 marking the 50th anniversary of the University's founding. She later commented: "We went into a packed ballroom where they introduced the alma mater for the first time. I felt very honored."

Bob Taylor was the first Freddie Falcon, introduced in 1950.

that was converted into another women's dormitory, known as Urschel Hall. By the late 1940s the Board of Control approved the modest size of the small cottage-style houses and construction resumed. By 1950, there were 22 units that became home to the new national fraternities and sororities.

The most pressing need was for male and married student housing. As the student "crunch" began to be felt in 1945-46, the trustees took a series of measures: remodeling of the football stadium to house 80 (later 150) men in rooms under the concrete stands; purchasing 50 trailers for married students and 15 pre-fabricated steel units each housing 20 male students; securing from the Federal Housing Administration wooden barracks made available by the closing of military bases, which altogether housed 1,000 men. Two trailer camps, one located where Jerome Library now sets and the other across Ridge Street in the vicinity of Overman Hall, were popularly known as Falcon Heights and Ridge Terrace respectively; in each, residents shared communal bathing facilities, one washing machine and a few pay phones. There was no running water, prompting the joke that "the only 'running water' was when someone made a mad dash from his trailer to the central pump on a cold morning." Among the off-campus buildings that the University purchased and converted to men's dormitories was one named Ivy Hall—more commonly known as The Hatchery, because it had previously been a chicken hatchery. Students said that a hatchery by any other name, still smelled like a hatchery. These makeshift dormitories, collectively known as "The Huts," frequently lacked adequate heating and other amenities. Lyle Fletcher, who joined the geography faculty in 1946 and taught at the University, said, "The huts were so cold it effected students' ability to write their term papers. Such circumstances required that many of them be given extensions."

In addition to these housing measures, the University also secured a mess hall from Camp Perry, which the military was liquidating. The building was moved to Bowling Green and became known as Commons. Four temporary buildings were also constructed to house several academic departments and to provide additional classrooms.

Falcon Heights and Ridge Terrace were two trailer camps that helped ease the post-war housing shortage.

The word "temporary" applied to most of the faculty as well. The expansion of higher education across the nation made it difficult to recruit and retain well-qualified faculty. In the immediate post-war years, much of the faculty was comprised of short-term appointees who lacked the essential qualifications for tenure-track positions at a university. Between 1940-41 and 1950-51, the number of full-time faculty increased nearly three-fold from 85 to 233, but the number holding doctorate degrees actually decreased from 55 to 50. It was argued at the time that the heavy reliance on temporary faculty did not reduce the quality of instruction, for many instructors had extensive teaching experience (mostly at the high school level) and were effective in the classroom. While all colleges and universities engaged in a desperate search for qualified faculty, the University's relatively low salary scale aggravated its competitive position. The University's chief in-state rivals—Kent State, Miami, Ohio University—had salaries that averaged $615 more than at Bowling Green; that was a considerable difference at a time when the University was offering starting assistant professors $3,700 and full professors were "topping out" at $5,500.

Prout was unwilling to address the salary issue, contending that it had to be deferred until funding became more stable. The University was operating on a tight budget, with student tuition and fees remaining the lowest in the state and appropriations from the Ohio Assembly failing to keep pace with expanding enrollments.

The growth of enrollments and the strengthening of liberal arts and business administration enabled the University to rationalize its administrative structure. The division of departments among colleges based on administrative convenience rather than disciplinary lines had outlived its usefulness. Acting on faculty recommendations, Prout in 1951 implemented the reorganization of the colleges. Inherent in this structure was a departmental responsibility to colleges and a strengthening of each college's stature. It also meant that the college of liberal arts would be preponderant, at least in terms of the number of departments and faculty. To assure coordination of academic programs, the office of vice president and dean of faculties was established.

The new structure put in place the basic disciplinary organization of the three oldest colleges that has endured, albeit with numerous changes and the establishment of additional colleges. With 16 of 27 departments being assigned to liberal arts, that college was divided into three divisions: humanities, social studies (later social sciences) and natural sciences. The reorganized collegiate structure included:

College of Liberal Arts:
Humanities Division:
English, foreign language, art, music, speech;
Natural Sciences Division:
biology, chemistry, engineering drawing, geography and geology, mathematics, physics;
Social Studies Division:
history, political science, psychology, sociology.

College of Education:
Education, graphic arts, health and physical education, home economics, industrial arts, library science.

College of Business Administration:
Business administration, economics, journalism, military science and tactics, secretarial science, business education.

These 27 departments underscored the movement toward greater autonomy for several disciplines: the splitting of the older dual disciplinary departments of chemistry and physics, history and political science, psychology and philosophy. Only geology and geography remained (to be divided a few years later). Also,

the military science and tactics department reflected the establishment of an Army Reserve Officers' Training (ROTC) program in 1948-49; this was followed by an Air Force Reserve Officers' Training (AFROTC) program in 1951-52 and a department of air science and tactics, which was also housed in the College of Business Administration. The ROTC and AFROTC programs proved popular, especially with the reinstitution of the military draft in 1948.

The growth of graduate programs necessitated a more formal administrative structure. Since 1936, the modest graduate offerings had been the responsibility of the Division of Graduate Instruction, which was administered by a graduate committee. This was sufficient to handle the programs of the eight departments that offered the Master of Arts degree (biology, education, English, foreign language, history, mathematics, social studies, sociology). After 1945, the graduate program expanded to include additional degrees: the Master of Education, Master of Science in education and Master of Science in business administration; by 1950, 19 departments were offering master's degree programs. This led in 1947 to the establishment of the Graduate School under a director, whose title four years later was changed to dean.

The expanding student body and the change of its character profoundly affected campus life. Symptomatic of that transition was the demise of the compulsory weekly assembly, which dated to the University's first year. It became impractical because of the lack of an auditorium that could house all students, but more importantly, student interest waned and attendance declined. To many students especially older ones, the assembly smacked too much of high school. As a result, Prout abandoned the assembly and the tradition quietly died.

The demise of one tradition was paralleled by the beginning of another: the strong Greek system. Building on the establishment of the first chapters of national fraternities and sororities during the war years, Greeks were firmly established as a center of social life by the early 1950s. In view of the greatly increased number of male students, it is not surprising that most of the new chapters were fraternities: between 1946-51, there were 12 national fraternity chapters established. During that same period, six national sororities came to campus. Thus by 1951, the University was housing 15 national fraternities and 11 national sororities. Prout took enormous pride in this development and was involved personally in Greek life. He frequently visited fraternities and sororities, often bringing with him gifts, including deliveries of firewood from the trimmings of campus trees. Not all of Prout's initiatives were welcomed; witness the "purity poles." James Galloway, class of 1950 and Student Senate president (and later a University administrator) recalled that Prout "didn't like it that every night you would find hundreds of fraternity guys hanging out on the lawn around the sorority houses … until the last minute when they dropped off their dates. So he put up light poles—everyone called them 'purity poles'—all around sorority row."

Greek activities, such as the Mud Tug, offered social outlets for participants and spectators.

[Alcohol] violations, of course, occurred, but they were relatively few and were handled by campus police. No attempt was made to control off-campus drinking.

To the administration, the most troublesome aspects of the changing character of students involved the use of automobiles and drinking. As early as 1944, the University prohibited student use of automobiles. The prohibition grew out of the increased number of students using cars and the lack of adequate parking facilities, as well as pressure from residents who complained about "joy riding" and about couples "petting" in parked cars. With many older and married students enrolling after the war, the policy became impractical and was amended in 1947, requiring cars to be registered with campus officials. Then in 1949, Prout presented more detailed regulations, including the provision that "unmarried women students … are not permitted to make use of an automobile in any manner except upon special permission of the Dean of Women." While intended to protect young women, that stipulation created absurd circumstances; a professor recalled offering a female student, burdened with a heavy load of books, a ride to campus on a cold

winter day, only to be told that she could not accept because it would be against the rules. To clarify matters, the board in 1951-52 changed the restriction on women in automobiles: "in any manner" was modified to "for social purposes." With respect to drinking, the University had always prohibited the serving or consuming of alcoholic beverages on campus. Violations, of course, occurred, but they were relatively few and were handled by campus police. No attempt was made to control off-campus drinking, but again this was not considered a serious problem. This all changed after the war, leading the Board of Trustees in 1947 to pass regulations that imposed fines, including suspension from the University, for drunkenness, bringing alcoholic beverages to campus or consuming them on campus. The University vigorously enforced these regulations, resulting in a number of student dismissals.

The University's *in locus parentis* policy to limit activities of women and to control drinking led to student unrest, which was manifest in several student strikes and demonstrations beginning in 1949. Veterans and other older students were in the vanguard of this movement, which paralleled similar protests for greater student rights at campuses across the nation. James Galloway recalled one of the protests: "The vets—who were 24-, 25-, 26-years-old at that time, remember—shut the campus down. Everyone went to [University Hall], sat down and closed the building. I went and sat down with the president, the deans of students and others. We worked it out." Over all, however, Prout did not handle the unrest very well, essentially scolding the students and warning of

The Changing Campus Scene

Despite the scant resources available for construction during the Depression, war and immediate postwar period, the University secured funding for some projects. This was a prelude to the considerable expansion of campus facilities during the 1950s.

During the late 1930s, the long-planned athletic complex, which had been initiated with the construction of the Men's Physical Education Building (Eppler South), was realized, thanks largely to funds from the Public Works Administration and Works Progress Administration, which were two of the agencies established by Franklin Roosevelt's New Deal program. The Women's Physical Education Building (Eppler North) and the since-razed Natatorium (located between the two physical education buildings), and the football field, located in the area between the present Education Building and Jerome Library, were completed. In 1938, the Board of Trustees purchased the brick house at the corner of East Wooster and South College (the present Popular Culture building) as a home for the University president. The following year, Kohl Hall, the first men's dormitory, opened.

Aside from the two small residential cottages that marked the first stage of what became sorority row, the only permanent construction during the war years was the Johnston Health Service Building, completed in 1942, which housed the University's medical service and a 32-bed infirmary. That facility helped the University secure the V-5 and V-12 training programs during the war, as did the purchase of 120 acres of land north of Poe Road that was used to construct a flying field, named Bricker Field in recognition of Governor John Bricker's role in securing funding. Also, the Falcon's Nest, constructed in large part by University funds, met the student's longstanding request for a student union.

In the late 1940s and the early 1950s, the temporary buildings accommodating the postwar enrollment boom gradually gave way to permanent ones, including the construction of a second science building (Overman Hall), Industrial Arts Building (at the airport), Fine Arts Building and Prout Chapel. The non-denominational chapel, modeled on the churches of the early settlers in the Firelands area, was constructed by a state appropriation for a music practice hall, supplemented by a gift from Sidney Frohman of Sandusky.

With the growth of enrollment, the University made a major commitment to residence hall construction. Between 1955-60, four new facilities were completed: the since-razed Alice Prout Residence Hall (for women), named for the late wife of the former president; Rodgers Quadrangle (for men), named for E. Tappan Rodgers, who in 1961 completed a record 23 years of service on the Board of Trustees; Founders Quadrangle (for women) with four separate residence halls, each named for a state official who had been instrumental in securing the 1910 legislation establishing the University; Conklin Quadrangle (for men), named for the former Dean of Students Arch B. Conklin. With the completion of these facilities, the University housed nearly 5,000 students.

Paralleling the dormitory construction during the late 1950s, three classroom-office buildings were added during the late 1950s: Hall of Music (West Hall), Home Economics Building (Family and Consumer Sciences Building) and South Hall. Memorial Hall, which included a new basketball arena subsequently named for Harold Anderson, was completed in 1960.

The most significant addition to the campus was the construction of the Student Union, which opened April 11, 1958; this met a longstanding need for additional cafeteria facilities, meeting rooms for faculty and student groups, and rooms for University guests. During this construction, a new configuration of the campus was determined to make it more enclosed and less centered on the original buildings. The old mall—Court Street's extension to campus that ended in a circle at University Hall—was removed. The streets and sidewalks were replaced by grass, trees and new cement walks. South Hall and the planned 10-story Administration Building (which opened in 1963), which were located at the two of the former entrances, reinforced the enclosure. To many, the University now looked like a campus.

---

dire repercussions from Columbus. He told the Student Senate in November 1949:

> *Misconduct of students on the various state university campuses in Ohio is resulting in a great downfall of public confidence in what is going on in these institutions. This lack of confidence is developing into a feeling of animosity in the state legislature toward the state universities, which is becoming a decided hindrance to these schools in obtaining sufficient state aid to meet operational costs.*

Prout was correct in terms of the political implications, but his seeming insensitivity to student concerns led to charges in the Student Senate that campus morale was at an all-time low. Such criticism was a bitter pill for a president who had committed himself to what would be later labeled "putting students first."

Beset by student unrest and entering his 11th year in office, Prout informed the Board of Trustees in 1949 of his decision to leave office as soon as a successor could be appointed. Unlike previous presidential appointments, the board undertook a national search and fully involved the faculty. Indeed among the eight presidential appointments in the University's history, faculty participation in this instance proved the most influential in that a faculty committee determined the finalists. After drawing up a list of qualifications including an unwritten one that the next president should have no present or past affiliation with the University, the board asked Prout to appoint a faculty committee to work with them in the search. As it worked out, the board deferred to the faculty committee to investigate candidates and to recommend a list of acceptable candidates. Headed by James Robert Overman, the nine-member faculty committee considered 100 candidates and eventually investigated the backgrounds of eight men. By June 1951, the committee had narrowed the field to three candidates whose names were submitted to the Board of Trustees. Resentful of the exclusion of candidates with a Bowling Green affiliation, the faculty committee asserted its independence by including Ralph G. Harshman, dean of the College of Business Administration, on its list. As anticipated, the board went "outside" in appointing one of the other finalists: Ralph W. McDonald. He assumed office on Sept. 1, 1951.

The appointment of the 58-year-old McDonald was significant not only because of the extent of faculty involvement, but also by the nature of McDonald's background. The faculty committee, comprised of eight faculty from Liberal Arts and one from Business Administration, added its own unwritten qualification: the next president should not come from a public school background, but should have experience at the college or university level and beyond northwest Ohio. When first reviewing candidates, the committee, following Overman's lead, wanted a president "in the academic mainstream" and rejected McDonald as too much an "educationalist" because he held a Ph.D. from Duke University in educational psychology and was executive secretary of the Department of Higher Education of the National Education Association (NEA). A couple members of the committee, however, thought highly of McDonald. In the spring of 1951, as several top candidates withdrew or proved disappointing in interviews, Paul Jones of the journalism department who had been

impressed by McDonald's administrative skills in running a large conference a year earlier, arranged for him to meet with the committee. Members of the committee were favorably impressed. Convinced that McDonald had a broad view of higher education and that his NEA experience enhanced his stature, the committee included him among its three finalists and its members, seemingly without exception, welcomed his appointment. His background and experience in higher education marked a significant break from the rather parochial qualifications of Williams, Offenhauer and Prout. Heinlen Hall, a member of the chemistry faculty who served on the committee, later remarked that its members assumed it was "time for a change, a time for a more rigorous administration, but I think it probably opted for too large a change, for too rigorous an administrator."

Ralph W. McDonald was named the University's fifth president in 1951.

Football's Greatest Moment: The 1959 National Champions

Doyt Perry, class of 1932, took over as head football coach in 1955 and immediately transformed a better-than-average team into an outstanding one. Over 10 seasons, Perry, who was elected to the National Football Hall of Fame in 1988, led Bowling Green to 77 wins, 11 losses and 5 ties. His 1959 team was the only unbeaten and untied football team in the University's history and was ranked the No. 1 Small College team in the final UPI poll. (The NCAA did not divide teams into divisions until 1978.)

That achievement was not expected. At the beginning of the season, Bowling Green was ranked 14th in the nation, while archrival Miami was ranked second. The season opener against Marshall University, set the stage for the season when Bowling Green won handily, 51-7, and set a record for the most points scored by one MAC team against another. The remainder of the season was just as magical, with wins against Dayton, Western Michigan, Toledo, Kent State, Miami, Southern Illinois, top-ranked Delaware and ending the season against Ohio University.

Perry took his fighting Falcons to the top of the charts in 1959.

In the final game against Ohio, the Bobcats led at halftime 9-0, and were hoping to mar the perfect season for the Falcons. Bowling Green took advantage of a fumble to score its first touchdown, making the score 9-7, and in the final quarter, Jerry Colaner intercepted a pass at midfield and raced 50 yards for what proved to be the winning touchdown"—resulting in a perfect season. Nearly 1,500 students and fans greeted the Falcons as they returned from Athens that evening. Ron Blackledge recalled that scene. "I remember the bus pulling into the union, and what a great feeling it was. It hadn't really hit us that we were undefeated, and we were the national champs. It was a great ride."

Indeed the contrast between McDonald and Prout was stark in every way: McDonald was a visionary who was determined to transform the University.

He was both brilliant and hard working. He was also remote, arbitrary and controlling. The reflections of several faculty of that era paint the picture of a complex leader.

Robert Keefe of the physical education department and longtime tennis coach said, "Oh boy, he was something else. He was an autocrat; he was a very strong individual, and when he was president he made all of the decisions. But I think he was very good for BGSU. He brought us out of the era of the teachers college into the era of the modern university." Joe Buford, who joined the geography faculty in 1948, recalled, "We went to Prout's exact opposite, Ralph W McDonald who was a solid, solid academic type and he shook up the University as no one has shaken it up since. … McDonald was cold … with most people, that was the impression you got."

Bruce Bellard agreed. "We went from the easy-going, flower-garden kind of things that Dr. Prout promoted … to a high-pressure, high-power political, work 16-18 hours a day. Dr. Ralph McDonald was the hardest worker that I have known in my career. … He worked 16 to 18 hours a day, lights were always on in his office. … He expected his people to work, he expected no deadheads." Amy Torgerson put it simply: "McDonald was a brilliant man, I think, a workaholic, and thought everybody else should be workaholics."

Sam Cooper and Robert Twyman underlined his accomplishments and shortcomings' Cooper said: "He was the scholarly academician type of president. He completely turned Bowling Green in a different direction. He was a tremendous hard worker. His administration, however, would have been referred to as dictatorial or almost tyrannical."

Twyman praised "McDonald [as] probably the greatest president we've ever had. … He was really a first-rate president. … He could not, however, delegate authority. McDonald would have done anything for the university to make it great. He even sacrificed himself." These comments underscore the difficulty of a balanced judgment on the administration of McDonald, "the flawed builder."

McDonald came to office at an opportune time when the "temporary" label on buildings and faculty was coming to an end and Bowling Green, freed from the exigencies of the previous 15 years, was at last in a position to fulfill the traditional mission of a university.

Bowling Green went literally from the bottom to the top among its peers; by 1960-61, its faculty salaries surpassed those at Ohio University, Kent State and Miami and rivaled those at the nation's leading universities.

The spiraling growth of the post-war years ended in 1950 when enrollment declined for a few years, before beginning a manageable annual increase through the remainder of the decade. The enrollment of 4,684 students in the first semester of 1949-50 marked the peak, and then over the next three years, it declined steadily, reaching 3,221 in 1953-54. The dwindling number of veterans accounted for part of the decline; also contributing to it was the University's decision to relieve the overcrowded housing conditions, which temporarily reduced on-campus accommodations. In 1954-55, enrollment began a steady upward growth, adding about 500 students per year through 1960-61 when it reached 6,229. Improved living conditions on campus made Bowling Green attractive to prospective students. In implementing the largest residence hall construction in the University's history between 1955 and 1960, the Board of Trustees consciously sought to balance the gender ratio, which had become disproportionately male-dominated. That objective was achieved: in 1960-61, male undergraduates totaled 3,013 while the number of females was 2,888. The biggest surge of students, a function of the higher percentage of female students, was in the College of Education, which regained its premier status, enrolling more students than the Colleges of Liberal Arts and the College of Business Administration combined.

McDonald envisioned that this more stable university would be a vastly better one. As the faculty shed its largely "temporary" character,

McDonald was determined to improve its quality. When he became president, only 22 percent of the faculty held doctorates, so the contracts of many temporary and part-time faculty were not renewed, and only well-qualified men and women were added. Moreover, many promising faculty who lacked a doctorate (or other appropriate terminal degree) were encouraged to resume graduate study; 22 faculty members responded by returning to graduate school, earning doctorates, and then resuming their teaching careers at the University.

Fundamental to recruiting and retaining faculty was addressing the University's low salaries. This had long been recognized as a problem, but McDonald, unlike Williams and Prout, made the upgrading of salaries a top priority. During his first year in office, he put into place the University's first salary schedule, which classified faculty not just by rank but by level of training within each rank and which also provided for a substantial increase in salaries. In addition to rewarding the best-qualified faculty, the schedule also exerted pressure on those lacking a doctorate to pursue that degree. This meant that the median salary at all ranks increased significantly: 25 percent for full professors, 15 percent for associate professors, and 8 percent for assistant professors. This compensation package—the largest percentage increase in University history—was covered by a reduction of approximately 30 faculty positions, mostly temporary, which was facilitated by the interlude of declining enrollments.

The faculty generally welcomed this upgrading of the faculty tied to a salary schedule. There were some critics, particularly terminal-master's faculty who resisted pressures to pursue doctorates and grumbled that the historic teaching mission was being neglected. Yet there can be no doubt that McDonald's scheme worked, for by 1960-61, the number of faculty holding doctorates had risen to 61 percent. Compared to their peers in Ohio and across the nation, Bowling Green faculty fared better in terms of compensation than at any time in the school's history. Bowling Green went literally from the bottom to the top among its peers; by 1960-61, its faculty salaries surpassed those at Ohio University, Kent State and Miami and rivaled those at the nation's leading universities.

An important element in strengthening the faculty was increased emphasis on research. In earlier years, many members of the faculty had engaged in research and creative works despite heavy teaching loads and the University's ambiguous position on its importance. McDonald placed emphasis on scholarly productivity in faculty recruitment, evaluation, tenure and promotion. To facilitate research, the standard teaching load was reduced from 15 class hours a week to 12, and faculty members with strong research records often had still lighter loads. These measures paid dividends: a survey of faculty productivity in 1959-60 showed that more than 100 books and articles had been published over the previous two years; in addition, creative work in music and art had become more prominent.

"McDonald was responsible for more of the buildings than anyone else. He was ambitious. ... He was a good planner. He could really figure out space, space arrangements and so on."

Fundamental to all aspects of academic enhancement during the 1950s was the dramatic expansion of the University Library's holdings. For two decades after its opening in 1927, the library was more than adequate to house a modest book collection, and its third floor was used for faculty offices and classrooms. During the 1950s, that space was converted to book stacks, and as the collection of books and journals increased, an addition was constructed to house those materials. Under McDonald's presidency and the efforts of Paul Leedy, who served as University librarian from 1944 to 1961, the number of books and documents almost doubled, reaching 330,000 by 1960-61 and the number of ongoing periodicals increased from 725 to 950.

The strengthening of the faculty and graduate education went hand-in-hand. During the 1950s, graduate enrollments increased by 65 percent, reaching a total of 328 students in 1960-61. The quality of graduate training improved, as the University eliminated a few programs

because of low enrollments or inadequate facilities; by 1960-61, master's degrees were offered in 16 fields.

Finally, despite the reservations of many faculty who felt he was pursuing a goal beyond the University's capacity, McDonald advocated establishing doctoral programs. In October 1960, the Board of Trustees authorized the president to begin planning for the doctorate in four fields (biology, education, English and speech). Believing that it was important to move deliberatively but also boldly, McDonald pressed for launching the first Ph.D. program the following year. The department of English was considered the strongest and the board approved its proposed Ph.D. program. Following favorable review by authorities in Columbus, the University launched its first doctorate in 1961.

Beyond the strengthening of academic programs, McDonald devoted much time to building the University physically. The University architect Jack Raney stated, "McDonald was responsible for more of the buildings than anyone else. He was ambitious. He would have made a good architect. He was a good planner. He could really figure out space, space arrangements and so on." Indeed, the campus was transformed during his presidency; $35 million was spent on construction of new buildings, renovations, improvements and the purchase of land. He envisioned the eastward development of the University, which led to acquisition of land beyond the old "eastern edge" of campus (near the present Jerome Library) toward where the football stadium now stands. Altogether, the campus nearly doubled in size, reaching 610 acres, excluding the 120 acres at the airport. McDonald was instrumental in the most dramatic transformation of the campus: the removal of the old walks and streets centering on University Hall—a move which enclosed the old campus in a natural setting and facilitated expansion by removing that entry as the "center" of the University.

McDonald also essentially designed what became the Joe E. Brown Theatre in University Hall; the large area under the auditorium (Eva Marie Saint Theatre) had originally been a gymnasium and then a recreational area that was used for student dances and other social events before the Student Union opened in 1958. It was McDonald's idea to convert it into a small

A Gala: The Golden Anniversary Celebration 1959-60

The theme of the University's year-long 50th birthday celebration–"Education Our Challenge, Excellence Our Goal"–reflected the expanding aspirations of higher education as it moved into a decade of expansion. Beginning with President McDonald's address to the University community in October, the many-faceted celebration reflected his vision of Bowling Green's role in society as well as his belief that "nothing was too good" for the University.

Five symposia throughout the academic year–focused on the humanities, business and education, the social sciences, the sciences and mathematics, and education–were meant to "stimulate thought and to spark the quest for knowledge." Before large audiences that attracted many people from throughout the region, the seminars brought to campus a number of nationally known figures including (among others) U.S. Supreme Court Justice William O. Douglas, humanities scholar Stringfellow Barr, literary critic John Ciardi, the president of Owens-Illinois Glass Company Carl R. Megowen, paleontologist George Gaylord Simpson, geophysicists Gerard Kuiper and Benjamin Howell, and education scholars Louise B. Ames and R. Freeman Butts.

The anniversary also celebrated the arts. The National Ballet of Finland, in its first American tour, gave three performances. To overflowing crowds, the famed contralto, Marion Anderson, appeared in concert and the renowned actor Vincent Price gave a performance honoring three giants of the arts. The theater department presented a series of productions, each dedicated to one of the five decades of the University's existence. The highlight was comedian Joe E. Brown's reprise of his Broadway performance starring in "Harvey," the popular comedy of the 1940s. It marked the last of the Holgate, Ohio native's some 1,600 performances playing the role of the tipsy Elwood P. Dowd whose closest friend was a six-foot invisible rabbit.

A convocation on May 19, 1960–the 50th anniversary of the signing of the legislation to establish a normal school in northwest Ohio–featured speeches by Governor Michael V. DiSalle and Harlan H. Hatcher, president of the University of Michigan, and the introduction of the University's new alma mater. It was a fitting culmination to a remarkable celebration.

> Written with the assistance of Jennifer Ricker

theatre, which was named for the Holgate, Ohio actor who had supported the University's theatre program and had starred in the silver anniversary production of "Harvey."

Although he was not especially interested in sports, McDonald considered a high-profile athletic program to be vital to an aspiring university. He believed that Bowling Green had to build on its reputation as a national power in men's basketball and to achieve comparable stature in football. He was instrumental in replacing Robert H. Whittaker who had been head football coach since 1941; his teams enjoyed a winning record (66 wins, 50 losses and 8 ties), but since Bowling Green joined the MAC in 1952 had not fared well, losing by lopsided scores to Miami and Ohio University. Doyt Perry was hired to replace him and immediately turned the Falcons into a nationally recognized football power.

The McDonald presidency thus marked substantial progress toward the realization of University status in fact as well as name.

McDonald seized the opportunity for expansion opportunity and provided a clear direction for the University. He was more a visionary than his predecessors and indeed than most of those who followed him into the presidency. He worked diligently and tirelessly to make that vision a reality.

Stuart Givens–who was hired by McDonald in 1952, taught history for 45 years, and authored the 75th anniversary history of the University–always considered McDonald to be Bowling Green's greatest president. When asked at the time of his retirement what he would say to McDonald in 1997, Givens said, "I would say to him, 'Look around and see what your dream has become. All of this is here because of you.' Speaking as a historian, I would have to say that he is the one who made Bowling Green a REAL university. Before that it was very much a teacher's college. He laid the foundation. Others have built upon it, expanded on it, but he is the one who made it all possible." ■

The Student-Faculty Revolt Against McDonald

The most momentous episode in the University's history marked the end of the presidency of Ralph W. McDonald. What began as a student protest in late March 1961 evolved into a student-faculty "revolution" which over the next three months captured the attention of the media throughout Ohio, led to intervention by the Ohio General Assembly and ended with McDonald's resignation.

These tumultuous events were not anticipated, but the grievances of students and faculty against McDonald had been building for a decade. The "revolution" is an important chapter in the University's history: it was a "defining moment" which was instrumental in the University's maturity.

Student indignation over stringent rules had led to the strikes and demonstrations toward the end of the Prout administration. McDonald, who regarded strict regulation of student life as integral to a first-rate education, tightened some rules, notably prohibiting student off-campus consumption of alcohol and "public displays of affection" (including the holding of hands on campus and "good night kisses" at women's residence halls). Such social policies were more restrictive than those at most colleges and universities. Bowling Green was typically considered the most conservative of Ohio's state universities. While students generally resented his rigid social policies, they supported McDonald's efforts to improve the University, including new residence halls and a student union. Recalling his work as student body president with McDonald, Albert E. Dyckes, class of 1953 (and later a Board of Trustees member) spoke admiringly of McDonald's goals to make "Bowling Green the Harvard of the Midwest" (the "stringent and subjective rules" notwithstanding), and his reliance on Dyckes to handle "student leader's tasks." For instance, after Toledo University students painted graffiti on the campus prior to a football game, McDonald called on Dyckes to make certain that Bowling Green students did not retaliate—a mission that Dyckes fulfilled.

To his faculty defenders, McDonald was a highly successful president (many regarding him long after the events of 1961 as the best in the University's history) whose leadership was undermined by irresponsible students and spiteful faculty. To his critics, "Black Mac" was an arbitrary and authoritarian president, whose policies ignored participatory governance and cost him the respect of faculty.

Early in his presidency, McDonald championed greater faculty involvement in governance. The Faculty Charter of 1949 was amended to enhance the authority of the University Senate and Faculty Council. Yet the system did not work effectively; the Senate barely functioned, and the Council served largely as an arm of the administration. Most faculty, even those who were generally supportive of McDonald, blamed him for not soliciting their advice. Sam Cooper of the physical education department, spoke for many colleagues: "He set up all the ways of involving the faculty and the students and so on in decision making. Then he would go ahead and do it his way anyway." The problem, as Robert Twyman of history put it, was that "McDonald could not delegate authority." Charles Barrell, who was the longtime chairmen of the political science department, said, "He had to make the decisions himself ... He had good ideas, but other people had ideas too. He just couldn't delegate talent. He consumed a lot of time making all these little decisions as well as big ones." On the other hand, McDonald's defenders, like James Robert Overman, the longtime faculty member and administrator, believed the underlying responsibility for failure rested as much with recalcitrant faculty. In his history of the University's first half-century, Overman acknowledged that "the failure of the machinery for faculty participation was undoubtedly the greatest weakness in President McDonald's administration," but he added, "The blame for its failure must be shared by the administration and faculty" exacerbated by "a lack of communication between faculty and President." In his view, faculty opposed to McDonald "were only waiting for a good opportunity to voice their grievances and demands" and that moment came in 1961.

The simmering student and faculty discontent erupted that spring. As he responded to the unfolding crisis, McDonald proved incapable of compromising, much less of understanding the concerns of his critics. He continued in a style of leadership that had brought major changes to the University, but was ill-suited for dealing with students, faculty, political leaders and the media in a politically charged situation. In sum, the "flaws" of the "flawed builder" undermined all that he had "built."

McDonald's lack of political acumen had been evident in May 1957 when he encountered the first substantial student protest of his administration. The University administration learned that members of Sigma Chi fraternity had been observed drinking at a fraternity-sponsored dance in Findlay. It demanded that the Interfraternity Council place the fraternity on probation. After the council duly did so, the administration then demanded the names of the men who had been drinking so that they could be expelled or suspended (the only sanctions for violating the no-drinking policy).

The council, with its vice president George Howick (who was later a faculty member at the University) playing a prominent role, passed a resolution condemning the University drinking policy. This protest triggered a one-day sit-down strike with about one-third of the students refusing to attend classes.

A nasty situation could have been avoided if he had remained at his home, met the students and respected their right to present grievances.

That night students organized a torchlight parade to the president's home where Howick was to present McDonald the resolution with a list of grievances. When the marchers reached the president's home, however, they discovered that McDonald had left the campus. At that point, student leaders lost control of the protest. With a number of non-students joining in, a large crowd gathered in front of the president's home at the intersection of South College Avenue and East Wooster Street, hanged McDonald in effigy and started a bonfire.

The protest held up traffic on East Wooster Street (which at that time was part of the major east-west Route 6 highway). Firemen put out the blaze, turned their hoses on the crowd, and several large trucks weaved through the crowd to break the jam. It took more than an hour before the normal flow of traffic was restored. It was an eventful middle-of-the-night confrontation.

The episode showed McDonald at his worst. A nasty situation could have been avoided if he had remained at his home, met the students and respected their right to present grievances. Moreover, McDonald retaliated immediately; the next day he expelled the student leaders. As Howick put it later, he was expelled "for leading a riot, which was not true ... but I did help to lead a torchlight parade." The 1957 confrontation, epitomized by the bonfire and the congested traffic on Route 6, became part of student lore, and each ensuing spring brought expectations of another "uprising."

After he entered the building, many students remained outside, chanting "We Want Beer" and singing "Old McDonald Had a Farm."

In spring 1961 an "uprising" occurred that had far greater ramifications. It began innocently enough on the unseasonably warm Sunday, March 26, when a spirited water fight among members and pledges of Sigma Chi fraternity attracted a large crowd of onlookers, estimated at 500 to 1,000 students. As more students doused each other with water, many formed a huge snake-dance line that twisted from campus into East Wooster Street and made its way to the front of the president's home, stopping traffic in the process. When McDonald left his home in mid-afternoon to attend a concert at the Student Union, he called for the students to disperse. They refused to do so and became increasingly unruly. Much of the crowd followed him on his 200-yard trek to the union. After he entered the building, many students remained outside, chanting "We Want Beer" and singing "Old McDonald Had a Farm."

Campus police arrived and tried to disperse the crowd. Elden Smith, dean of students, also appealed for dispersal, but was greeted by water-filled balloons, one which hit him. The police raced to apprehend the balloon thrower, while most students started shouting, "Founders! Founders!" and headed to the nearby women's residence at Founders Quadrangle to get more students to join in the protest. The doors to Founders, however, had been locked, preventing any more women students from leaving the building.

Most of the crowd returned to the front of the union where at 5:40 p.m. McDonald appeared at a second-story window and once again asked the students to disperse. By that time, he had called the state highway patrol to break the traffic jam on East Wooster Street and, as he spoke, state police officers took up positions in front of the union. McDonald briefly engaged the students, responding sarcastically to a question about the controversial firing of a fraternity housemother, but overall he seemed to regard the day's activities as innocuous. That did not mean, however, that he disregarded the need to bring order to a chaotic situation. As the demonstrators then moved "in hoards"—some to the football stadium, some to downtown Bowing Green and then back to campus—police began to sweep the campus. Police apprehended a number of demonstrators, stopped and searched cars, and eventually arrested seven students, who were released after the University declined to press charges. The crowd finally dispersed by 10 p.m. when women students had to return to their dormitories.

The incident was "news," with an Associated Press wire story calling it a "near riot." The University administration, however, insisted it was "frivolous fun." McDonald stated:

> " *The demonstrations didn't amount to much. It began as a water fight, which we have on campus occasionally. I have never seen a more peaceful group. Chanting in protest at so-called childish rules was just in fun. ... It was just a peaceful group with smiles on their faces.* "

A University spokesman added that the "the chant of 'we want beer' was just for fun. ... We would hate to see anyone attach a seriousness of purpose to the demonstration because it wasn't there." While the incident received considerable coverage in the *Toledo Blade* and *Bowling Green Sentinel-Tribune*, the *BG News* parroted the administration's position, barely covering the events: "The story is brief ... hardly a riot." Yet the disrespect shown McDonald and other authority figures, like Smith and the police, suggested something more than a superficial spring outing might be in the works. That was evident during the next three days—a short week of classes before the beginning of Easter Break.

Demonstrations resumed the next day--Monday, March 27—but the protest became more focused. The frivolity of "We want beer" and "Old McDonald's Farm" was replaced by a spontaneous class boycott and sit-down strike and led by day's end to a list of student grievances. As the Associated Press reported, "Displaying banners carrying such slogans as 'We Want Freedom,' hundreds of BGSU students began a classroom boycott today." Indeed that morning some 300 students boycotted classes and staged a sit-down strike in front of University Hall, where by the afternoon of another warm day, close to 2,000 students eventually gathered. Leaders planned a demonstration in dining halls at the dinner hour, but that was called off because patrolmen were in the buildings. Instead, a large number of students marched down Wooster Street and ran wild through the business district, tying up traffic. The city police ordered them to stay on sidewalks, but when one student strayed into the street, he was clubbed over the head by the police chief and arrested for disorderly conduct. That incident triggered a march back to campus and the setting of several bonfires and another burning of McDonald in effigy.

Meanwhile, a large number of students assembled at 5 p.m. outside the union for a scheduled forum, which featured several speakers who generally supported the students' goals but urged restraint and peaceful protest. Among the speakers were Dean of Men Wallace W. Taylor, the star football player Bernie Casey and student body president-elect Clark Tibbits. Attracting the most attention were Sherman Stanage, an assistant professor of philosophy, and Rev. James Trautwein of St. John's Episcopal Church. Stanage praised the students for their orderly behavior, saying peaceful protest was the key: "Bowling Green can grow up at this moment if you will let it." Trautwein, describing himself as a "mediator," volunteered to bring student grievances to the attention of the administration. Moreover, he cast the protest in moral terms, like the civil rights movement, and suggested civil disobedience to bring change. At the conclusion of the meeting, the assembled students voted to boycott classes the next day.

The administration remained dismissive of the students' position. Dean of Students Smith stated that they had no single overwhelming complaint, but rather a collection of individual grievances. "It's gotten to the point where the students are looking for a cause," he said. In fact, a number of grievances, stirred in part by the Stanage and Trautwein speeches, were stated that evening, including women's dormitory restrictions, the ban on "public displays of affection," and infringements on freedom of speech, press (alleged censorship of the *BG News*) and assembly (all student meetings having to be cleared by the administration).

As the second tumultuous day ended, McDonald declared a state of emergency and ordered students to stay in their rooms the next day unless they were going to or from classes. The city police detained 15 students overnight; all were released the next day.

The Tuesday, March 28 boycott was largely successful, with several hundred students refusing to attend classes. Nearly all students defied the order to remain in their rooms and a large number again gathered in front of the union. Many of them burned copies of the *BG News* with its pro-administration account of the Sunday incident. Still others published and distributed a one-page sheet titled "Desire to Be" which identified the "basic problem[s] of the University to be the lack of freedom of the individual" and the lack of "open communication."

"Desire to Be" called for allowing the *BG News* to become a voice of student concerns and student government to be more representative of

Students hold a "sit-out" in front of the Student Union on March 28, 1961 in protest to McDonald's stringent rules.

student opinion. Significantly, the manifesto also appealed to the faculty to assert itself:

" The faculty, being the heart of any university, ought to have the controlling voice on policies impinging on the educational process and on their rights as individuals. Policies ought never to be something handed down by the administration. "

Meanwhile, leaders of fraternities, sororities and residence halls met and agreed to a list of "the 10 most serious grievances" which were they planned to present at a Student Council meeting that afternoon and to McDonald afterward. Student Council, however, demurred, saying it would consider grievances at a meeting two weeks later. Speaking to a large crowd gathered outside the union, Student Council President Keith Trowbridge tried without success to explain the council's position, which added to the impression held by many students that the administration controlled student government. Then McDonald appeared and, to jeering and booing, ordered the students to disperse. Instead the crowd gained more followers as it moved to another part of campus, where amidst speeches and chanting, McDonald was again hanged in effigy and

another bonfire was lit. At about 8:30 p.m., McDonald proclaimed an emergency, whereupon the police moved in to disperse the crowd, and the third day of protest ended quietly.

The next day, Wednesday, March 29, marked the last day of classes before Easter vacation, which from the administration's viewpoint was fortuitous, because it was assumed that the break would erode the momentum of the protests. Yet the mood on campus suggested otherwise. As they left, many students carried signs proclaiming: "Home for Riot Recess" … "We Want Reform" … "We Are Fugitives from BGSU."

As a deterrent to further unrest, the administration took a strong stand against alleged instigators. Forty-three students were "detained" from leaving, with Dean of Men Taylor stating: "This is not a witch hunt. We feel it's a counseling situation." Eight students were dismissed and another 30, pending further inquiry, faced possible suspension upon their return. Yet the crackdown had the opposite of its intended effect, for it reinforced the plans of some students to carry their case to hometown newspapers and to state officials.

That same day as students were leaving campus, faculty discontent came into the open when an untenured junior faculty member publicly questioned the University's commitment to free speech. The occasion was a meeting of faculty called by McDonald, who spoke at length about the demonstrations, which he described as misguided protest against reasonable rules. They had been instigated by about 200 students, mostly freshmen, and supported by outsiders from other campuses. He exhorted faculty to impress upon students the importance of civility when they returned to campus. As was customary at faculty meetings under McDonald, there was no invitation for comments and McDonald prepared to adjourn the meeting. Then Sherman Stanage—in what would become a

As students left for Easter vacation, many carried signs proclaiming, "Home for Riot Recess," "We Want Reform," and "We Are Fugitives from BGSU."

legendary moment in the "revolution"—stood and challenged McDonald's leadership. Stanage's recollection was similar to that of faculty who were present:

" I remember very distinctly what I said immediately after Mac's speech. I stood up and said, 'President McDonald, I rise to speak in behalf of a vanishing ideal of Bowling Green State University—the ideal of free speech.' "

McDonald demanded that Stanage stop, until finally, amidst considerable commotion in the audience, he said that "those who wish to stay and listen to Dr. Stanage can do so, but the rest may leave." Stanage went on to defend the students and to call for faculty leadership: "The students have asked us for bread, and we have given them stones. … All they want us to do is listen to them and to their concerns."

This proved a decisive moment of the McDonald presidency. It linked faculty and student grievances. It assured that the protest would resume after the break. In fact, both student leaders and anti-McDonald faculty were active over the next week, strengthening their positions.

During the three days of agitation, media coverage had sided with the administration and regarded the protest as, at best, frivolous and, at worst, disruptive. The *Sandusky Register*, for instance, editorialized that students should stop worrying about rights and start thinking about responsibilities, while a columnist in the same paper suggested: "A new motto has gone into force at BGSU—'Why study when you can riot.'" The *Lorain Journal* wrote, "If these young people are this immature, they are not ready for college and its privileges." An editorial in the Northwest Signal, published in Napoleon, told students, "If you don't like it [at Bowling Green], go home!" and went on to defend the administration: "Old fuddy-duddies that we are, we agree, clear out the beer drinkers and sexpots" (neither of which had been evident in the demonstrations). Less strident editorials in two major newspapers—the *Cleveland Plain-Dealer* and *Columbus Dispatch*—also blamed protest on irresponsible students.

That tone continued in most of the press, but the two papers closest to the scene—the *Toledo Blade* and *Bowling Green Sentinel-Tribune*—offered more balanced appraisals and

became steadily more critical of McDonald. This reflected to some extent their direct contacts with disaffected faculty and students, but also by the palpable sense on campus of an administration that was losing control. Thus, a March 29 *Blade* editorial "Cold War at Bowling Green" (which was reprinted in the *Sentinel-Tribune*) suggested the unrest was perhaps symptomatic of a serious problem. Observing that "[It was] notable that Bowling Green State University is the only one of Ohio's six state-supported Universities where boisterous demonstrations have occurred," the editorial concluded:

" But if what has taken place at BGSU is a reflection of an underlying resentment by the student body over what it may regard as abnormally strict irritants placed by the administration in the path of normal campus life, then the matter should be looked into before it sparks more serious uprisings that could detract from the main purpose of the university. "

Convinced that serious dissent was minimal and that public sentiment was behind him, McDonald continued to take a hard line. On April 1, he sent a rather testy letter to the parents of students, contending that the University's regulations on student conduct were integral to a quality education. Reiterating the argument that a handful of students were responsible for the demonstrations which others had joined "just in fun," McDonald wrote:

" For many, many years, Bowling Green State University has been recognized for the traditional decency, sobriety and sincerity of its students. The regulations of the University are intended to preserve this tradition … It is only natural that some students would seek admission to the University in order to obtain the benefits of our excellent educational program and campus life but would resent the very policies and regulations which have made possible the benefits they wish to share. "

Over the next week a number of those angry students—whom McDonald sought to marginalize—actively pushed their grievances. A number of them sought interviews with local news reporters and wrote letters to editors in hometown newspapers. Their efforts had some effect. The *Lorain Journal* gave prominence to a letter from a Bowling Green student who responded to that paper's critical editorial: "we merely want the right to voice our opinions … a lot more would be accomplished if the public would question the happenings at the college, instead of immediately condemning the students." Most notably, after interviewing Bowling Green students from the Akron area, the influential *Akron Beacon-Journal* reported that their grievances centered on undue restrictions that prevented them from demonstrating their responsibility; they saw themselves "conducting a real fight for principles."

"This whole thing smacks of juvenile delinquency. I would be much more impressed if you were down here arguing for improvements in the curriculum."

Meanwhile, a couple dozen students, mostly from the Cincinnati-Dayton area, took their case to Columbus. The first such overture occurred within hours after the students left campus, when Sue Ericksen, a junior from Dayton who had just been expelled, phoned the office of Governor Michael V. DiSalle, whose spokesman told her that the governor had no power to intervene. Privately, Di Salle sent McDonald a letter expressing confidence in his leadership, adding: "I have not wanted to intrude since I felt if you were in need of assistance you would call." Ericksen and others then targeted the education committees in the General Assembly. Over Easter weekend, newspapers throughout Ohio reported that Ericksen, Marge Lewis, a freshman from Cincinnati, and other students were heading to Columbus on Monday, April 3. Trying to head-off a potentially embarrassing situation, McDonald urged the students to return to campus so they could discuss their grievances with him.

In a significant step, the students ignored McDonald and met with members of the General Assembly. On April 3, the House Education Committee granted an informal hearing with 12 students; because students could be expelled for being named in newspaper accounts unfavorable to the university, only the name of the group's spokesman, Tom Brundett, a freshman from Tipp City, was released. They found the committee divided, one member being quite hostile, stating, "This whole thing smacks of juvenile delinquency. I would be much more impressed if you were down here arguing for improvements in the curriculum." Other members were more receptive. Ethel Swanbeck, a Republican from Huron, and Stanley Arnoff, a Republican from Cincinnati, left the committee hearing to phone McDonald "to inform him of the situation and ask him to see the students and hear their grievances." Although the House Education Committee took the position that it could not act in the situation, McDonald could not ignore the pressure from two of its members.

Meanwhile, another student mission to the Senate Education Committee—led by Ericksen and Glenn Schmidt, a January 1961 graduate from St. Mary's—was markedly successful. It gained a meeting with the committee's influential chairman, Senator Ross Pepple, a Republican from Lima. Pepple sympathized with the students and told them to make a list of grievances and spoke of an investigation if students cited examples of unfair treatment. An investigation, Pepple added, "would be a powerful weapon."

The students' serious demeanor in their meetings with legislators undercut the perception of immature and unruly protestors. The next day's *Cleveland Plain-Dealer* headlined it story of the students' accomplishment: "Bowling Green Students Get An 'A' in Lobbying."

McDonald was taken back by the students' initiative and their favorable reception. He was also stung by an editorial that same day in the *Bowling Green Sentinel-Tribune*. The paper, which rarely ran editorials, had a brief one on its first page. Titled "Campus Tension," it blamed both student demonstrators and the university administration for "arbitrary actions and poor communications," but notably sympathized "in some respects" with student complaints and chastised the administration:

    ❝ *Any administration invites trouble when it fails to encourage a free flow of ideas on which should be a two-way street of communications. Without freedom, misunderstandings multiply.* ❞

Under these pressures, McDonald adopted a conciliatory stance, telling an interviewer that the students' going to Columbus was "quite all right." He praised the orderly way they had conducted themselves and conceded that some of their criticisms were valid. In a remarkably disingenuous statement, he even claimed credit for telling the legislators that they should talk with the students:

> " *I felt that the problems felt so keenly about the students should be taken up with the legislators since they were already in Columbus. I am sure the students can help me understand problems that may exist which have not been called to my attention.* "

He closed by saying that he always "welcome[d] the opportunity to discuss problems or questions with any student or group of students."

McDonald followed with a conciliatory letter to all students as they returned to campus. He invited them to send suggestions to Student Council on ways to build a "better place in which we can all study and work together," promised his "very careful consideration" of Student Council recommendations and extended a "welcome" to his office to discuss "any problem or anything at all in which I might be able to help."

These gestures, however, did not end the administration's effort to marginalize the demonstrators not only as immature but also, at best, average students. On April 6, it was announced that a total of nine students had been dismissed and five others placed on probation; moreover, they were identified as nearly all freshmen with a "C or below" average.

Despite his efforts, McDonald's leadership was increasingly tenuous, beset by challenges from within the University and from Columbus. The Stanage challenge had encouraged a number of dissident faculty to become more aggressive in criticizing McDonald, with a number of them contacting the *Toledo Blade*, which in editorials on April 2 and 6 (reprinted in the *Sentinel Tribune*) charged that McDonald ruled with "a heavy fist" with the complicity of an indifferent of Board of Trustees. While McDonald might be addressing some student concerns, "there is the more serious matter of faculty dissatisfaction." A university needed to respect "the academic integrity and independence of its faculty."

Then Senator Pepple intervened. While not ruling out an investigation of student complaints, he took another more immediate tact. On April 5, he proposed legislation to increase the number of the members on the Board of Trustees from five to nine (later modified to seven), with the provision that at least two members had to be University alumni. Noting that he had been told that 90 percent of faulty sympathized with the students, Pepple contended that increasing the size of the board was a way of providing fresh perspectives. In words that sounded gratuitous to McDonald, Pepple stated, "I thought it might be a good idea to increase the board. This could give McDonald more help and better advice." What Pepple did not say—but what was clear in his advocacy of an enlarged board—was that the McDonald administration, abetted by a Board of Trustees that rarely questioned his actions, had lost support of students and faculty. Pepple stated that his proposal would not be a "positive guarantee" against future demonstrations, but "it would tend to create a more smoothly working university."

... Most notably in a letter to the Senate Rules Committee, [McDonald] lashed out at his critics and questioned their integrity—a strategy guaranteed to backfire.

Seeing the Pepple proposal correctly as a direct challenge—in effect a legislative vote of confidence in his leadership—McDonald fought a solitary struggle against it. Over the next two months, he lobbied against Pepple's proposal, making it what would eventually be the final point of contention in his struggle to hold power. In retrospect, it would have been wiser for him to accept an enlarged board without comment.

In fighting against the Pepple proposal, the problem for McDonald was that it seemed reasonable on its merits, regardless of the situation on campus. As a result, the measure gained substantial support. As Pepple and other advocates pointed out, it would: (1) bring Bowling Green's

Board of Trustees into line with those at other state universities all of which had at least seven members; (2) broaden the board's geographic representation, which at that time was drawn from a remarkably small area within northwest Ohio (Bowling Green, Cygnet, Norwalk, Tiffin and Findlay); (3) assure a voice for alumni who had no representation on the board; (4) provide fresh perspectives to a board on which four of the five members had served for at least 15 years. Pepple's bill drew the support of Representative Charles Kurfess of Bowling Green, a number of alumni who testified before the Senate Education Committee, and editorials in the *Toledo Blade* and *Bowling Green Sentinel-Tribune*. In a searing editorial, "A Most Devoted Board," *The Blade* indicted the cozy relationship between McDonald and the Trustees:

> " *It's little wonder that Dr. McDonald hails the present BGSU board as one of 'most devoted boards of trustees that could possibly be found.' How could he regard this tight little group otherwise? It could hardly function more smoothly from his point of view if he had handpicked its members. Time and again, the trustees have shown no inclination to do more than rubberstamp Dr. McDonald's high-handed actions … The best hope for improvement of the BGSU climate rests in final passage of the bill … to add two more members to the board.* "

In his opposition to the Pepple proposal, McDonald avoided the arguments of its advocates. Instead, most notably in a letter to the Senate Rules Committee, he lashed out at his critics and questioned their integrity—a strategy guaranteed to backfire. It was a "shot-gun" argument. First, the damaging, nationwide publicity of "student demonstrations … widely publicized as mob riots … [was] entirely false," McDonald contended it originated with the irresponsible reporting of the *Bowling Green Sentinel-Tribune*. Second, the demonstrators were a "group of 200 to 300 unruly freshmen, who had worked themselves into a noisy frenzy by their own disorderliness; the idea of having 'grievances' occurred to them as an afterthought." Third, Pepple, instead of recognizing the frivolous nature of the protest, "greeted these students warmly, gave them his encouragement … [and] introduced a bill presumably to serve the purposes for which they

were demonstrating." Fourth, the bill in turn drew the support of the "*Sentinel Tribune*, which has never missed an opportunity to treat the University unfavorably," joined now by "disgruntled alumni … a local leader and his close associates in one of the political parties, who have sought for many years to get their selectees appointed as University trustees … [and] four or five disgruntled faculty members who had encouraged student demonstrations." Finally, in an unfortunate closing, McDonald impugned the character of the *Sentinel-Tribune*'s editor Paul Jones, as a disgruntled former employee of the University. (Ironically, as a member of the presidential selection committee in 1951, Jones had played an important role in recruiting McDonald). Beyond his indictment of his opponents, McDonald—in an exaggerated claim—maintained that passage of the bill would encourage student unrest at campuses throughout the state.

Besides appeasing students, McDonald also reached out to faculty, saying he would approve reactivation of the Faculty Senate as a self-governing body.

Paralleling his campaign against the Pepple bill, McDonald took a conciliatory stance with students and faculty, but after years of being ignored, many were skeptical of McDonald's sudden openness. A *Blade* editorial described it as "only a strategic withdrawal by a President under fire."

For their part, student leaders, following the counsel of faculty supporters to avoid demonstrations, focused their grievances on more principled issues than off-campus drinking and "public displays of affection," and to work through student government. Their enhanced credibility put pressure on the more established voices of student leadership—notably Student Council and the *BG News*—to demonstrate their independence of the administration. Indeed the *BG News* conceded that it had been "wrong at the time" in understating student dissatisfaction and "had no evidence" to support its report (based on administration sources) of "outside agitators " at the protests. At a three-hour meeting on April 13, Student Council, which had been criticized earlier for its deliberative approach to student grievances and with its leadership now in full support, passed a resolution of complaints, which centered on five points:

» *liberalization of automobile regulations (eliminating the "double jeopardy" whereby a student convicted of a traffic offense in civil court was also subject to additional penalties by Student Court);*

» *recognition of the integrity of the press (accepting as final the* BG News *editor's decision on comment and coverage);*

» *liberalization of class attendance policy (doubling the number of "cuts" allowed);*

» *reform of the rules governing women students (reviewing and simplifying the large "inconsistent and trivial" body of regulations);*

» *improvement of administrative attitudes (establishing better relations with students, including the role of campus police).*

As the resolution passed, President Trowbridge expressed confidence that McDonald would be "very receptive." Indeed McDonald stated his "complete agreement with the [resolution's] principles, aims and objectives." He promised early Board of Trustees' approval on the "double jeopardy" reform and that his administration would address the other issues promptly.

Besides appeasing students, McDonald also reached out to faculty, saying he would approve reactivation of the Faculty Senate as a self-governing body. On April 11, the Faculty Council, whose membership included eight elected faculty members as well as McDonald and two other administrators endorsed that proposal (and also passed unanimously a resolution expressing confidence in McDonald and the Board of Trustees). The next night in what constituted the formal reactivation of the Faculty Senate, a representative group of 11 faculty presented McDonald a statement that set forth the objective of a fully autonomous Senate playing a prominent role in University governance. McDonald stated his unequivocal support of the proposed objectives. A second open meeting on April 17,

attended by over one hundred associate and full professors, elected Robert Twyman, chairman of the history department and vice chairman of the Faculty Council, as president *pro tem*. Twyman foresaw, with "a free Senate serving as a deliberative body, we will have a good balance at the University." A *BG News* editorial thought it "curious" that faculty were pushing for power so close to the students' protest, but was gratified that this underlined a common goal.

Despite his conciliatory gestures, McDonald could not quiet criticism. The *Columbus Dispatch* ran a four-part report on the Bowling Green situation (which was reprinted in the *Sentinel-Tribune*). Written by the *Dispatch* education editor and based on interviews with faculty, administration, students and other sources, the articles emphasized the extent of student and faculty discontent and wrote sympathetically of the call of both groups for a more participatory system of governance and commitment to freedom of expression. Acknowledging the significance of the students' initiatives, a number of faculty were quoted to the effect that "they are fighting our battle." Overall McDonald emerged as a leader who in his zeal to build the University had sacrificed communication with faculty and students and had manipulated or marginalized representative bodies.

Emerging as leaders of the dissident faculty were Richard Carpenter and Howard Brogan, both of the English department, and Grover Platt of the history department. They took their complaint of suppression of freedom of speech to the Ohio Civil Liberties Union, which began an investigation. The Bowling Green chapter of the American Association for University Professors (AAUP) also pressed the case against McDonald and on May 19 it requested that the national AAUP office investigate the McDonald administration in the face of "continuing deterioration of faculty-administration relations." The dissidents redoubled their efforts to make their case with newspaper reporters and editors. Carpenter, for instance, in a letter to *The Blade* education editor,o called attention to McDonald's continuing effort to "drive a wedge" between his faculty "loyalists" and those, like Carpenter, who were being portrayed as "subversives." Pointing out that the dissidents included some of the most experienced and respected faculty members,

Carpenter said, "One would hardly think that was a subversive group." In addition, the dissidents sought to meet with members of the Board of Trustees, succeeding in one case with James C. Donnell of Findlay, who was chief executive officer of the Ohio Marathon Oil Corporation and who became sympathetic to the faculty and student grievances.

Then on Saturday, June 3–the day before spring commencement–the University fired Stanage. Summoned to the office of Vice President Kenneth McFall, Stanage was informed that his contract would not be renewed beyond the 1961-62 academic year. McFall told Stanage that the dismissal was based on his failure to develop "an outstanding program of instruction in religion." Previously, Stanage, who had been on the faculty since February 1959 and was chairman of the two-person philosophy department, had received favorable comments on his work from academic officers, including McDonald.

The tone of coverage and ensuing editorials and letters to editors turned decidedly against McDonald.

Word of Stanage's firing spread across campus. It electrified students and faculty and impacted commencement. A number of graduating seniors phoned *The Blade* and the offices of legislators to protest the firing. On June 4–the day of their graduation–a letter from "129 Seniors in Mourning" protested the action of the "high-handed tyrant" McDonald and his "hatchet-man" McFall for dismissing Stanage, because he had "the courage of his convictions" and then justifying that retribution "by questioning his professional ability."

Many faculty members (including some McDonald supporters) agreed with Stanage that his dismissal was "retaliatory for speaking out for students' rights." Twenty faculty met the afternoon of June 3 to protest Stanage's firing and to voice their lack of confidence in McDonald's leadership. They quickly drafted a "no-confidence" petition to the Board of Trustees. Within 24 hours, they gained the support of 60 faculty members, including the

chairmen of five departments. Charging that Stanage was "being punished for the temperate exercise of free speech," the petition closed: "this latest in a series of vindictive punishments for expressed differences of opinion had caused a complete loss of confidence by us in President McDonald's administration."

Newspapers throughout Ohio reported on the firing, and the story was picked up by the major news services. The tone of coverage and ensuing editorials and letters to editors turned decidedly against McDonald.

As the criticism mounted, the Board of Trustees met in a special session on the evening of June 5. In a 45-minute meeting, the board did not consider the petition and heard only the administration's rationale for the dismissal. It voted unanimously in support of the administration. *The Blade's* editorial the next day indicted the board for its irresponsibility: "Without so much as pretending to consider merits of the petition, [the board] in a hastily called special session, fell right into line with the decision of President McDonald. … Four of the Trustees admitted they had not even studied the petition."

In addition to the board's backing, McDonald was also supported by a second petition, which circulated on campus June 5-6. It read:

> *[The signers] deplore the unfortunate results of the resolution recently signed by 60 faculty members and express complete confidence in the president's ability and the ability of other administrative officers and the University Senate to deal internally with the situation currently confronting the university.*

A total of 115 faculty including 17 department chairmen, and 27 administrators signed the petition. The fact that nearly twice as many faculty had signed the pro-McDonald petition as had the "no-confidence" one suggested that McDonald enjoyed the support of most faculty. An accurate measure of faculty sentiment, however, was very difficult. Dissident faculty charged that many colleagues had been pressured by their chairmen to sign the second petition and that the chairmen had been pressured by deans. While some anecdotal evident supported those charges, what cannot be ignored is that McDonald still had substantial faculty backing.

Robert Keefe of the physical education department, who was chairman of the Faculty Council in 1960-61, commented many years later:

This revives some bitter memories. ... The faculty was divided and you were forced into being either for McDonald or against McDonald. I am not ashamed to admit that I was for McDonald, because I thought he was good for the University, not that I am saying he was perfect and I think he made some serious mistakes.

It was that dual character of McDonald's leadership that led a minority of faculty to take, as one of them put it, "a middle of the road position," which seemed generally to be supportive of student grievances and sympathetic to Stanage's plight, but not to endorse "no-confidence" in McDonald. With 175 out of 225 faculty having endorsed one of the petitions, it would seem that about 50 faculty members fit into the "middle of the road" camp.

Regardless of the faculty sentiment, McDonald's presidency was unraveling. The Board of Trustees' unswerving support of McDonald came under criticism from editorials in newspapers, which had earlier been supportive of McDonald. For instance, Napoleon's *Northwest Journal*, which had strongly indicted student protest two months earlier, now called for state investigation, asking what "mystical power" McDonald has over the board; "What does he have that BGSU can't get along without?" The *Springfield Daily News* stated that the situation warranted examination by AAUP: "No state can afford to let one of its great universities become hostile to the free expression of ideas."

Meanwhile, the dissidents pressed their case that free speech was on the line. In an interview with *The Blade*, Stanage stated that the board's failure to listen to dissenting faculty was "shocking" and that the legislature and public needed to know that McDonald was "personally responsible for conditions that would not be accepted at most respectable institutions." He justified his public campaign on that basis: "Academic freedom is the reason I have decided to bring the termination of my contract into the open instead of quietly looking for another job." Along with several supporters, Stanage secured a meeting on June 7 with two members of an increasingly embattled board–Carl H. Schwyn and John

Ernsthausen–who listened to their complaints. Out of that meeting emerged the board's decision to convene another special meeting on Sunday, June 11 at which representatives of the faculty would be invited to speak. Referring to the faculty representatives as "fine men," Schwyn stated, "We have to bring them (faculty and administration) together again."

About 65 people crowded into the room for the Board of Trustees meeting. A message from Representative Charles Kurfess called for the board to make every effort to resolve differences to avoid a situation "which might invite official state attention."

He remained to the end a leader of remarkable certitude – arrogance if you will – that ill-served him when confronting criticism.

Critics and supporters of McDonald were allocated equal amounts of time. The dissident faculty, with Grover Platt as their principal spokesman, toned down the rhetoric from their petition a week earlier. This tactic was driven by the show of faculty support for McDonald and the clear determination of the Board to reconcile the parties. Rather than demanding the reinstatement of Stanage, Platt proposed that a seven-member member committee be appointed to investigate the dismissal and to issue a report that would be binding on all parties. "No-confidence" gave way to reconciliation, as Platt denied any intent to destroy the McDonald presidency. Stanage praised McDonald's work in strengthening the university and pleaded that faculty be allowed to help in the endeavor. On the other side, the pro-McDonald petition was formally presented with comments by University librarian Paul Leedy and Donald Bowman of the physics department, who both emphasized the breadth of support across disciplines and faculty ranks. They emphatically denied that coercion accounted for the strong show of support; McDonald's record of accomplishment had earned "the respect and admiration" of faculty and staff. The June 11 meeting lessened tensions, but its implications for the future of the University were unclear, at least

McDonald, who departed as a "broken, dispirited man," severed all ties with the University and did not even return for the dedication of the residence hall named for him.

until the regularly scheduled meeting scheduled for Saturday, June 24.

Working tirelessly to reach some compromise were a handful of "middle of the road" faculty, with Twyman as *pro tem* senate chairman in the vanguard. He met with all board members, persuaded McDonald to take "the fire and brimstone from his speeches," and urged faculty leaders on both sides to seek some common grounds. Yet events had probably overtaken such efforts. A quarter-century later, Twyman recalled the futility of his mission:

“ *Eventually [McDonald] got mad at me too … Both [faculty] sides assumed I was on the other side. The radicals accused me of being too conservative, and the conservatives accused me of being radical … [M]y own effort was not very successful and I lost a lot of friends.* ”

Indeed by the time of the June 24 meeting, events in Columbus determined the fate of the McDonald presidency. By his own definition, McDonald suffered a loss of confidence when the Ohio General Assembly enacted the Pepple Bill. On June 7, the Senate had voted overwhelmingly (31-1) in favor of increasing the Board membership. Then on June 21, the House of Representatives followed suit, passing the bill unanimously (112-0). Governor DiSalle said that he would sign it into law. This constituted a devastating defeat for McDonald who had fought against the bill, literally putting his credibility on the line. In an editorial, *The Blade* spoke directly to the causes and consequences of this momentous measure:

“ *The troubled academic atmosphere at Bowling Green has been given further recognition in Columbus … It does offer an all important opportunity to get at a primary cause of the University's difficulties: a weak board of trustees … which permitted an alarming situation to develop … by turning over to an arbitrary president virtually all of its policy-making decisions. [This law] gives BGSU's trustees a new mandate to re-establish effective control over the University and to resolve a destructive dispute.* ”

At the Board of Trustees' June 24 meeting, McDonald—to the astonishment of most of those in attendance—accepted the inevitable and resigned as president. His lack of political acumen—notably

in the badly timed and unjustified dismissal of Stanage and the unrelenting opposition to an enlarged the Board of Trustees—led to a self-inflicted loss of credibility. The signs of an accommodating McDonald during the last weeks of the spring semester were misleading. He remained to the end a leader of remarkable certitude—arrogance if you will—that ill-served him when confronting criticism.

That attitude was manifest in a letter that he sent to faculty and staff, which blamed his resignation and the concomitant harm to the University on a handful of misguided faculty.

“ *I am confident that many of the faculty members responsible for these events were acting in good faith and had no intention to do such serious damage to the University or to me personally. … Only a very few of our colleagues—probably less than a dozen—either shared the motives or envisaged the damage that has been to the university by recent events.* ”

McDonald also called William Day, state editor of *The Blade*, and said that he held Day and *The Blade* "personally responsible for his problems and for his decision to resign."

Members of the Board of Trustees reflected similar bitterness. Alva Bachman of Bowling Green issued a stern warning to faculty: "Anyone who doesn't want to comply and cooperate in building a University … I am ready to accept his resignation this minute. Either he gets on and joins with the purpose we are dedicated to promoting or else he gets out." E. T. Rodgers of Tiffin, who that spring was completing the longest service on the Board in history (22 years), criticized *The Blade* and *Sentinel-Tribune* for unfair coverage, claiming that some editorials had been written by dissident faculty, and Senator Pepple for introducing his bill at a time of turmoil. John Ernsthausen of Norwalk added, "It would be a dark day for Bowling Green if the resignation were interpreted as a victory for a minority of faculty or for student rioters."

McDonald refused to be a "lame duck" and during the remaining 10 weeks of his presidency, he remained in control, settling some scores in the process. On the day of his resignation, the Board of Trustees announced the appointment of Ralph Harshman as Acting President, but McDonald made three important administrative changes at the same time: McFall, whose reputation had been undermined by his role in the Stanage firing, was "relieved of his academic duties" to become assistant to the president; Leedy, director of the library and a prominent McDonald supporter, was appointed to the newly created position of provost, and Donnal V. Smith, assistant to the president and former president of the New York State Teachers College at Cortland, was named dean of students, replacing Elden T. Smith, who had resigned to become provost at Ohio Wesleyan University.

McDonald's bitterness was subsequently evident in his dismissal from their administrative posts of two of the chairmen—Howard Brogan of English and Charles Young of education—who had signed the dissident petition. Questioned about the action in a television interview, Trustee Bachman labeled Brogan "a trouble maker from the moment he set foot on campus." Finally, in an act that underscored the need for a more responsible Board of Trustees, McDonald also added $400,000 to the University payroll, as

he awarded generous increments to selected administrators and faculty. At a time when beginning faculty salaries were about $6,000 and the president's salary was $24,000 and the average 1961-62 increment was $500, McDonald provided increases of $3,000 to 20 people, $4,000 to another eight and $5,000 to the top three. The most generously rewarded faculty and staff were McDonald supporters.

A divisive figure until the end, McDonald's supporters saw him departing as a "broken, dispirited man" while critics saw only an "arrogant, vindictive man." In accepting his resignation, the Board of Trustees granted McDonald a one-year leave of absence. He spent the next year in Washington, D.C., and planned to return to Bowling Green as a professor in 1962-63. The board, however, decided that his presence on campus would be disruptive and made clear he would not be welcomed. So McDonald severed his ties with the University. When a residence hall was named for him, McDonald refused to return for the dedication ceremony. ■

John F. Kennedy visited campus as part of his campaign tour.

1961-1982
A Maturing University

For Americans, the decade of 1960 began with a sense of promise that the nation was capable of addressing problems of social and economic inequality. The election of the 42-year-old John F. Kennedy as president in 1960 personified a new generation assuming leadership.

It was an auspicious time for higher education, which was held in high regard as helping to guide public policy as it experienced a decade of spiraling enrollments driven by the arrival of the "baby-boomer" generation beginning in the mid-1960s. Kennedy's call for national service—"Ask not what your country can do for you, but what you can do for your country"—inspired young men and women, especially college students, leading many to join the Peace Corps, which Kennedy established in 1961. They participated in "freedom rides" into the segregated South and engaged in

other forms of protest on behalf of civil rights of African-Americans and other minorities. Students also worked on behalf of recognition of their rights as students and became engaged in the revived women's movement and the rise of environmentalism. The sense of purpose soon gave way to deep divisions over the war in Vietnam. By the late 1960s, America seemed to be "coming apart"—to borrow the title of one book on the decade's turmoil. Bowling Green, like other universities and colleges, experienced the promise, the political tides and disappointments of the decade.

For the University, the decade began with confronting the aftermath of the turmoil that forced the resignation of Ralph McDonald. The Board of Trustees decided to undertake a national search for a new president. In the interim, it appointed Ralph G. Harshman, former dean of Business Administration, as acting president. This was a welcomed choice. Harshman, a member of the faculty since 1936 who had served 14 years as the first dean of the School of Business Administration, enjoyed wide respect among faculty, having been among the candidates recommended for the presidency by the faculty search committee at the time of the McDonald appointment. The board soon dropped the "acting" designation from the 68-year-old Harshman's title to make clear that he enjoyed its confidence and should not be restricted in exercising presidential prerogatives. It facilitated Harshman's capacity to achieve his most important objective: the restoring of campus morale and a sense of direction to the University.

In another important act, which reassured the university community, the board established a broadly based presidential screening committee chaired by the board's president J. C. Donnell. Appointed in November 1961, the committee included Harshman and another administrator, three senior faculty members (carefully selected to represent the three factions in the McDonald controversy), two alumni and three members of the Board of Trustees. Its representative character, except for the absence of student membership, made it a model for subsequent searches.

As the search progressed over the next 18 months, Harshman's efforts at healing were unquestionably successful. James Robert Overman, his longtime colleague and author of the University's history from 1910-1963, observed that the "confidence of all concerned in his ability, broadmindedness and sense of justice enabled him to quiet the troubled waters and to turn the thoughts of the University community from the grievances of the past toward the promises of the future."

Harshman, however, needed to confront the "grievances of the past" by dealing with the legacy of McDonald's presidency. Toward that end, he promoted greater faculty participation in university governance and delegated greater responsibility to vice presidents and deans.

More importantly, at his urging, the Board of Trustees' addressed the sources of the faculty and student discontent. It appointed a Faculty Study Committee of 11 faculty members and a Committee on Student Affairs, with 16 members drawn from faculty, administration and students. These committees made major recommendations, which were endorsed by the Board of Trustees and substantially implemented. The Faculty Study Committee recommended a decentralized administration and a Faculty Senate, which would be representative of all faculty, would be faculty-led, and would be the "faculty voice" with substantial authority to frame policy and make recommendations to the president and board. The report of the Committee on Student Affairs focused on relaxing restrictions on student conduct, giving students a greater voice in determining those regulations and taking measures that would assure the integrity of the *BG News*.

Beyond addressing the underlying issues of the movement against McDonald, Harshman and the board also confronted the arbitrary personnel actions of McDonald's last months. McFall returned to the position of vice president, which he held until his retirement in 1975. The board rescinded the dismissal of Sherman Stanage as an assistant professor of philosophy, and reinstated Howard Brogan and Charles Young as department chairmen. The $400,000 increase in the salary budget, driven by the large salary increments

As president, Ralph Harshman reassured the campus community after the McDonald controversy.

awarded to relatively few faculty and administrators, triggered criticism not only on campus but in the Ohio General Assembly. Thus, in March 1962, the board approved a large-scale readjustment of salaries, reduced the salaries of 75 faculty and administrators by a total of $56,000 and increased the salaries of 74 others by nearly $30,000. These reassuring measures meant that by the time a new president was appointed in 1963 the University was moving to "the promises of the future."

William Travers Jerome III, the dean of the College of Business Administration at Syracuse University, was named the University's fifth president, taking office on September 1, 1963. At age 44, Jerome was the youngest president in the University's history and he brought an impressive academic background. A magna cum laude graduate of Colgate University, he earned master's and doctorate degrees from Harvard University and had taught at Middlebury College before going to Syracuse University in 1953 where he had been dean since 1958. Jerome was especially interested in international education and had helped establish the first and only business school in Colombia, under the joint auspices of Syracuse University and the U.S. Agency for International Development.

Jerome was selected from among 140 candidates for the Bowling Green presidency. After an extensive 16-month search, the search committee recommended four finalists, each of whom were visited at their home institutions and then had come to Bowling Green briefly

William Jerome saw the University's potential for growth.

to meet with selected administrators, faculty and students—a more open process than earlier searches. Moreover, all four finalists—in addition to Jerome—Frank E. Duddy Jr., president of Westminster College (Utah); Paul Frederick Sharp, president of Hiram College; York Willburn, director, Bureau of Government Research, Indiana University—brought impressive academic credentials.

Art Professor Harold Hasselschwart designed the University mace that was unveiled at President William T. Jerome's 1964 inaugural ceremony.

From the beginning of his administration, Jerome—aptly described by a Syracuse colleague as having a "big booming voice to go with a fairly monumental physique"—envisioned the building of what he called "a maturing university" that was committed to a broadly conceived obligation to addressing society's problems. This was reflected in the theme of his September 1964 inaugural ceremony, "The State University: Creator or Conformist?" The academic processional marked the unveiling of the University mace, which was designed by Harold Hasselschwart of the art faculty. In his address, Jerome challenged faculty to develop an atmosphere which would foster great teaching and genuine scholarship and to expose students to foreign cultures, to underscore the power of ideas, to remind them that "in today's world, dreams and faith and brave fellowship still have a revered place" and to provide them with the "skills required to become successful doers." He lamented the "imbalance between society's commitment to the physical sciences and its commitment to the social sciences and humanities."

To Jerome, he was coming to a "university that very few people knew about, kind of out in the sticks to put it bluntly." That reflected a certain patrician quality, which alienated some faculty and townspeople. He seemed unduly critical at times of the University; as one faculty member said he "put his foot in his mouth and said things that he later regretted." On occasion, the bluntness was necessary. Upon being hired, he and his wife made it clear that the presidential home (the present Popular Culture building) "did not meet our requirements in any sense." After some consideration of building a home

Changing Campus Scene

The building boom of the 1950s continued into the 1960s. By the end of that decade, the campus had taken on the essential dimensions that exist to the present. As planned shortly after Jerome became president, the initial priorities were for a new library, a complex of science buildings on the north side of Ridge Street (life sciences, mathematical sciences, psychology) and residence complexes to accommodate the expanding study body: McDonald Quadrangle (1962); Harshman Quadrangle (1964); Kreischer Quadrangle (1966), and Offenhauer Towers (1971). Three of these facilities honored former presidents. It was fitting that the fourth recognized Edwin Kreischer, who retired as vice president of finance in 1965 after 20 years of service and had been instrumental in obtaining legislation that permitted universities to issue bonds to fund buildings, including residence halls.

The Jerome Library, science complex, together with the Business Administration and Education buildings, were funded by the state with additional support from the federal government under the Higher Education Facilities Act. Since its completion in 1967, the library stands as the University's most distinctive structure, thanks principally to the Akron-based sculptor, Donald Drumm, who "forever changed the face of this campus, through the startling exterior of its Library."

Bonds financed not only the residence halls, but other non-academic construction as well: the Student Services Building, the Student Health Center, the Ice Arena, the football stadium, the intramural playing fields and other athletic facilities, which were named for longtime coaches: Warren Steller Field (baseball), Robert H. Whittaker Track, Forrest Creason Golf Course, Cornelius (Mickey) Cochrane Soccer Field, Robert J. Keefe Tennis Courts and intramural playing fields. The two oldest residence halls, Williams Hall and Shatzel Hall, were converted into offices for academic departments in 1964 and 1966 respectively; during its last years as a residence hall for males, the aging Shatzel was affectionately known as "the hole with a soul."

During the 1970s, the pace of construction lessened, but there were several important additions: Business Administration Building, Technology Building, the Hollis and Marian Moore Musical Arts Center, the (Nick J.) Mileti Alumni Center and the Student Recreation Center. Renovation became increasingly

Jerome Library was one of the structures added to the campus during the '60s and '70s that changed the face of campus.

important, including major overhauls of the three oldest classroom buildings (University Hall, Moseley Hall and Hanna Hall), with the latter including the remodeling of an auditorium into a film theatre, named in 1976 the Dorothy and Lillian Gish Film Theater, a project led by Ralph Wolfe of the English department. The old library was converted into offices, including those of the president and provost, the Faculty Senate meeting room and an art gallery; the building was named the Kenneth H. McFall Center in honor of the emeritus vice president. With the construction of a new exercise facility between the North Gym and South Gym (where the Natatorium had stood), the three buildings were named in 1981 the Eppler Complex in honor of Gertrude Eppler who headed the Women's Physical Education Department from 1943-69. The "oldest building" on campus, in terms of its origins, was originally a one-room schoolhouse from Norwalk, Ohio. Donated by Frank Linder, the 100-year-old "Little Red Schoolhouse" was dismantled and rebuilt at its present location near the Education Building. Its collection of pre-1940 educational materials attracts about 1,000 visitors per year, mostly school children.

Ray Browne, along with his wife Pat, introduced the study of popular culture to BGSU and the world.

on campus, the University purchased a recently constructed residence on Hillcrest Drive on the west side of town, which served as the presidential residence for the next 42 years. Although some persons questioned moving the home two miles from campus, few challenged Jerome's point that the 25-year-old cramped home had outlived its usefulness, especially considering the social functions expected of the president.

What soon impressed Jerome about the "university in the sticks" was its enormous potential for growth. While he essentially continued on the path that McDonald had started, Jerome differed from McDonald in that he saw his role as encouraging ideas and initiatives. Where McDonald had been controlling, Jerome was open. As he began his second year at Bowling Green, Jerome told entering freshmen, "There is a reputation which I covet for this University more than any other. This is the reputation for innovation, the reputation for a campus where students and faculty alike are blessed with an imaginative spirit, a zestful spirit."

Karl Vogt, who came to Bowling Green in 1968 as an assistant to Jerome and became dean

of the College of Business Administration, said: "One thing about Bill Jerome is that he could really generate a high level of enthusiasm. ... Bill in many respects was a dreamer, a person who could generate great enthusiasm for something, but then it was up to the individual to translate that into some kind of action." Indeed Jerome was the "dreamer" who wanted to encourage the ideas of other. He later reflected:

" *It was exciting to see that with any encouragement at all, the [University] would grow. You found people who wanted to do things. I think of [Richard] Lineback and his philosophy index. This is now internationally known. I remember Dick coming in and talking to me about his idea; he needed a few thousand dollars. This is a fantastic idea, go with it; we'll find the money. Of course I remember with great fondness, the start of the center for popular culture. So I didn't have to do much there other than say to Ray Browne go with it, it's something that's exciting. I remember Dave Elsass having a dream of bringing that little red schoolhouse here. That was an exciting thought to me. It was done after I left, but in a sense the idea, the generation of that was something we thought about for a long time.* "

So two distinctive academic enterprises—the Philosopher's Index and the popular culture program, which in 1973 became the first department of its kind in the country and also spawned the large popular culture library—were launched in part because of Jerome's support; the school house stands as one of the distinctive features of the campus.

Another one of his enthusiastic endeavors was on behalf of the construction of the Ice Arena. The story is told how after the design for the building had been drawn up, a faculty member convinced Jerome that it needed to include curling facilities, which led Jerome to undertake a hurried visit, with architects and others in tow, to visit an ice arena in Ontario; this resulted in curling becoming part of the Ice Arena. As Carl Hall of the art faculty put it, "He had found that was a good idea, then why not do it? Get it pushed through and do it. And that's kind of the way he ran things."

Jerome also helped to fulfill the dream of Duane Tucker for a building to house WBGU-TV. Tucker, who joined the faculty in 1959, was

Basketball's Greatest Moment: The Victory Over Loyola, 1963

For much of early 1963, Loyola of Chicago had perhaps the most talented college basketball team in the land. When the season ended in March, Loyola was in fact the best of the best, winning the NCAA national championship with a 29-2 record.

But several weeks earlier, on a cold winter's night in February, the Ramblers were not even the best team in Wood County.

Loyola was loaded with great talent, including four of whom would later be drafted by the National Basketball Association. They came into Anderson Arena undefeated at 20-0 and ranked second in the nation.

Bowling Green, however, had an outstanding team of its own, led by two of the greatest players ever to wear the orange and brown - Nate Thurmond and Howard "Butch" Komives. Despite the weather outside, Anderson was cooking inside. Every seat was filled, and public address announcer Jim Hof implored students to squeeze closer together so more could get in. At one point so many students were pushing against the big plate glass windows at the front

entrance that one of the windows gave way. It was fortunate there were no serious injuries.

Up in the northeast corner of Anderson, nearly two dozen Loyola fans kept up the chant: "Ramblers! Ramblers!" But sparked by Komives' deadly shooting early on–he scored 25 of his 34 points in the first half–the Falcons continued to pull away after intermission. At some point in the second half, we didn't hear the Loyola fans any more.

The final score, 92-75, accurately reflects BG's domination. For at least one night, on Feb. 16, 1963, no team in the country would have beaten the Falcons' lineup of Thurmond, Komives, Wavey Junior, Elijah Chatman and their teammates.

Thurmond and Komives went on to play professionally for many years in the NBA. Thurmond, in fact, would later be named one of the 50 greatest players in NBA history. But they would never forget, and neither would the capacity crowd who saw it, the game that ranks as perhaps the greatest in the history of BGSU basketball.

> Tom Walton '65

---

key when the television station went on the air in February 1964 from studios in South Hall, broadcasting five hours a day and reaching no farther than Wood County. Plans were for a larger studio in University Hall, but Tucker, with McFall, thought that a new building was necessary; it was unclear whether the University would provide such funding, but as Tucker recalled, "Jerome liked the idea and soon the Board of Trustees decided it was a good idea so … away we went" with the construction of a 10,000-square foot building on Troup Street. A grant from the Department of Health, Education and Welfare helped fund the home of WBGU-TV (known now as the Tucker Center for Telecommunications in honor of Duane and Margaret Tucker). This facility permitted expansion of programming and of service to a broad region, as well as providing training for generations of students.

Jerome was committed to international education and supported the initiatives to provide opportunities for students to study overseas. In 1961, the romance languages department began a program of yearlong study in Madrid, Spain. A program in Tours, France followed. In 1969, the German Department launched it study abroad

at Salzburg, Austria. The College of Business Administration later began a summer program in Nantes, France. All of these programs still exist, and over the years have been supplemented by other opportunities that today literally span the globe, including programs in Russia, Ghana, Italy, Jamaica, Japan and South Africa.

Not everything under Jerome was spontaneous. Jerome had his own vision for the University. Unlike McDonald, he solicited advice from others and delegated authority. Not all change had to bear the president's identity. He fashioned a tight administrative system. Given the dramatic expansion of the University during his tenure, the growth of the administrative was quite modest. When Jerome took office, there were four top administrative positions (provost, vice president, dean of students and treasurer/business manager), which he transformed into three vice presidencies: vice president for academic affairs and dean of faculties; vice president for research and financial affairs, and vice president for student affairs. In 1964 Provost Paul Leedy noted early in Jerome's term, "You as President have delegated more authority to me as provost than the office ever had before." In a gesture that was well received generally, Jerome made nearly all administrative appointments from within the University, including his three vice presidents: Stanley K. Coffman, academic affairs and dean of faculties; B. D. (Bobby) Owens, research and financial affairs; James G. Bond, student affairs.

Augmenting the three vice presidencies, Jerome also established the Office of Institutional Research and Planning, the Office of Development and the Office of Research Services—all of which addressed priorities in a time of expansion. The establishment of the Ohio Board of Regents (OBOR) in 1963 to coordinate the expanding system of higher education made planning an institutional imperative. OBOR's state master plan called for the University enrollment to reach between 15,000 and 30,000 students. Its requirement that state universities prioritize and justify capital improvements led to the Office of Institutional Research and Planning. Soon the Board of Trustees approved plans that gave priority to a new library and a science complex as well as additional residence halls and athletic facilities. A considerable building boom resulted in the University taking on the essential dimensions that endure to the present.

The Office of Development reflected Jerome's conviction that the university needed to concentrate on private contributions, which led to various initiatives, including the launching of the Parents Club, Presidents Club and Falcon Club, and the University's first major fundraising campaign in 1966. By that time, the Alumni Association was reorganized and became engaged in generating alumni contributions.

The Office of Research Services addressed the importance of supporting research for faculty, provided internal funding through the Committee on Research and also encouraged and coordinated applications for external grants.

It was indeed a time of expansion. When Jerome took office in 1963, University enrollment stood at 8,238, including 7,700 undergraduates and 538 graduate students. By 1970, enrollment had grown by 67 percent, reaching 13,782; the number of undergraduates had increased by more than 4,000 and graduate students by 1,500. This paralleled the largest increase of full-time faculty in the University's history, going from 274 to 695 between 1963-70. This brought a reduction in faculty-student ratio from 27 to 1 in 1963 to 18 to 1 in 1970. The growth of graduate curriculum

was marked by the launching of Ph.D. programs in biology, educational administration, psychology and speech in addition to the inaugural doctorate in English.

The graduate program in psychology soon became nationally recognized for its work in the industrial-organization area centering on the scholarship of Robert Guion, the clinical area under John Exner and the "pure" research best represented by John Paul Scott, who joined the department in 1965 and was subsequently named Ohio's first Regents Professor. To recognize other outstanding research faculty, the Board of Trustees in 1970 established the title of University Professor (later Distinguished University Professor) to be conferred on faculty whose scholarship gained international recognition and ranged beyond one discipline.

Jerome generally gained the respect and support of faculty. Carl Hall later remarked, "Jerome had a very good personality and was adept at working with people." Nowhere was that trait more evident than in his relationship with faculty leaders. As he assumed office, the Board of Trustees approved the Faculty Charter with its provisions for a stronger and representative Faculty Senate. In 1964 Grover Platt of the history faculty was elected the first chairman under the new governance document, which he had been instrumental in drafting. Politically astute, Jerome made a determined effort to reassure the faculty of his commitment to faculty governance. His tactics bewildered some observers, even if they understood his reasons. Ashel Bryan, the longtime benefactor of the University who served on the Board of Trustees from 1968-76 commented, "Then comes Bill Jerome, the committee type. He appoints a committee for everything. That was important that they get everybody involved." Robert Twyman of the history faculty spoke somewhat disparagingly of Jerome as "sort of good for the times, because the faculty was feeling its oats and wanting to run things, and so he kind of let them." Jerome also gave strong support to the Faculty Senate's call for a sabbatical leave program and gained Board of Trustees approval; it was not until the mid-1970s, however, when the state legislature permitted state funds to finance leaves, that a faculty improvement leave program could be established.

Faculty respect for his leadership was evident when OBOR stipulated in 1967 that all state

universities were to convert the quarter-system academic calendar. Many faculty were upset with OBOR's assumption of such authority. Speaking to a large general meeting of the faculty, Jerome, who shared those concerns, called for faculty not to press the issue, which they accepted. At the same time, Jerome could at times act arbitrarily himself, most notoriously in ignoring a search committee's recommendations and appointing a vice president whom the committee had rejected.

While Jerome was not notably "student-oriented" in the sense of being present at many student gatherings, he enjoyed respect among students generally and worked effectively with their leaders. Alumni of that era speak of Jerome's "infectious grin … speeches at difficult times … [and] his understanding of our problems." Forty years after their graduation, the class of 1968 established a scholarship in Jerome's honor, in recognition of his "bold leadership, commitment to student and faculty learning, and personal statesmanship." Jerome was bound to that class by the national tragedies that occurred prior to the 1968 commencement: Robert F. Kennedy

had been assassinated during exam week, and two months earlier Martin Luther King Jr. was assassinated. Americans of all ages were left dispirited and despaired. Jerome considered canceling commencement, but two class leaders—President Edward Sewell and Chief Justice of the Student Court Bob Spence—met with him and said that Kennedy would have wanted the University to go forward. Jerome agreed, with the stipulation that both Sewell and Spence were to mention Kennedy in their remarks. It turned out to be a moving commencement ceremony, appropriate for a troubled time.

In the turbulent '60s, student life blended the "normal" with unprecedented level of "activism." Fraternity and sorority life remained vibrant; two new Greek traditions were established in 1964 with the first Phi Kappa Tau "Bed Race" and the Beta Theta Pi "Beta Little 500."

On the athletic front, new playing fields facilitated an expansion of intramural sports involving Greek and independent teams; by 1970, approximately 6,000 students participated in 29 sports. Both the major sports of the era,

Class President Edward Sewell was one of the speakers at commencement in 1968.

which remained strong competitively through the early 1960s, gained new facilities. In 1960 the basketball team moved its games from the Men's Gym (Eppler South) to Anderson Arena–named for Coach Harold "Andy" Anderson within the new Memorial Hall. Anderson's 21-year career as coach ended with the triumphant 1962-63 season, a MAC championship and an invitation to NCAA Tournament in which Bowling Green won its opening game against Notre Dame before losing to the University of Illinois. On Oct. 30, 1965, the football team played its final game on the field (between the present Jerome Library and Education Building), which had been its home since 1937. For the 1966 season, the team moved to the newly constructed 22,500 seat-capacity football stadium with the field named for Doyt L. Perry, who retired as coach after the 1965 season to succeed Anderson as athletic director. Meanwhile, another sport, which would rival football and basketball in popularity, took root in 1964 when a group of students launched a club hockey team and five years later, with the construction of the Ice Arena, it was elevated to intercollegiate status.

Students in general felt gratified by their education at Bowling Green and now look back fondly on a time of demanding classes and broadening of perspectives. John Schumm, class of 1967, recalled:

> *Most of us were from northwest Ohio and were a conservative breed. Meeting people of different religions and races was new. The dorms were filled with many discussions about politics and religion ... Academics ruled. Students took their subjects seriously. Remember that mom and dad received your grades and you did not want to disappoint them. Flunking out was a no-no! It was a social disgrace.*

Although the majority of students, like other Americans, were relatively content and stayed on the political sidelines, the "discontented minority," in the words of a 1970 American Council on Education Report, "are among the brightest, most experienced, widely read and articulate young Americans." Keying student activism was the objective of being recognized as responsible adults.

The long-standing question of serving alcohol on campus found greater acceptance, as the Student Council in 1967 called for selling 3.2

beer on campus (Greek and residential groups had authority to serve 3.2 beer at off-campus functions). Eventually the Board of Trustees, with Jerome's lukewarm support, approved by a five-to-three vote the sale of 3.2 beer in a designated area of the Student Union. Under further pressure from students to bring policy into accord with state law, the Board of Trustees in 1970 further liberalized its policy on alcoholic usage on campus, and drinking in residence halls and "happy hours" became commonplace.

The most significant changes affected the status of women. The "dress regulations" quietly ended that specified "shorts, Bermudas, jeans, slacks, etc." could not be worn in classrooms, offices, or dining rooms. Female students who married no longer had to inform the administration immediately or face automatic withdrawal from the University. Student demands for liberalizing residential housing policy were more controversial. The University gradually modified its requirement that all undergraduate women and all freshman and sophomore men to live on campus. Provisions for women's hours–mandating the time when women had to be in residence halls–were modified and then eliminated in 1968.

Students also called for "open houses" and the elimination of "calling hours," which limited the "entertaining" of "men callers" to women's residence hall lounges at specified hours. In 1969 nearly 250 students staged a sit-in in Rodgers Hall to demand "open houses" on Friday and Saturday nights and Sunday afternoon with the right to close room doors. The protest continued with a forum in front of Williams Hall where Student Council President Nick Licata called for a massive student presence at the Board of Trustees meeting later that day. Nearly 800 students descended on the meeting, and when the board president called for questions, Licata took control of the microphone; whereupon, Jerome and members of the board walked out. In the end, the administration placed a number of students involved in the sit-in on probation, but also agreed to allow two "open hours" per week with the approval of the residents but with "doors open and lights on." Not surprisingly, student leaders pressed for still more liberal policies, specifically for "open visitation" and for coed housing, which were becoming increasingly common at universities. Partly to forestall large numbers of students moving off-campus, the board authorized the first coed residence hall (Kreischer Darrow in 1971-72) and student determination (by floors and wings) of residence halls for 24-hour, 12-hour, or "lounge only" visitation arrangements.

Students were successful in pursuing other objectives, notably recognition of a greater role in administrative decisions, through less confrontational means. Underlying student grievances was a sense of the Student Council's "irrelevance to the university governance process" as its officers stated in 1969. The *BG News* described student government as "a hoax … an intricate, complex and highly efficient system of diverting students from getting anything of true value accomplished."

[The Vietnam War] divided Americans more deeply than any war in history, and nowhere were those divisions more evident than on the nation's campuses.

As Jerome and many faculty recognized, students saw an imbalance between the authority of the Faculty Senate and that of the Student Council. Beginning in 1965, the Faculty Senate became more open to requests from Student Council, including inviting the council president to attend senate meetings, considering requests for support of bills passed by the council, and agreeing to the seating of four undergraduate and two graduate students in the senate with full voting rights. Student leaders also pressed for the use of teaching evaluation forms as a part of the tenure and promotion process, which was endorsed by the Faculty Senate and by 1970, began to be adopted. Also, students urged non-voting student membership on the Board of Trustees, which Governor James Rhodes had suggested as a statewide policy; in 1970, the board invited student representation at its meetings.

Although President Jerome was supportive of the right of dissent, his tolerance was tested in a prolonged and contentious encounter with the *BG News*, which adopted an outspoken and uncompromising editorial policy and increasingly used what many readers considered obscene language. In June 1969 several hundred faculty and students signed a petition to Jerome protesting the newspaper's editorial bias and journalistic license and questioning whether the University should continue its financial support. The Student Publications Committee defended the paper as reflecting the urgency and temper of the times. On Oct. 3, 1969, the *BG News* changed its long-time masthead from "Serving a Growing University since 1920" to "An Independent Student Voice." In March 1970 Jerome threatened to cut off funding at some point in the future because, "for the life of me I can't see how a student newspaper can justify being subsidized by the very persons it chooses to vilify." The *BG News'* stridency was typical of student newspapers of the era, which prompted some to propose control of editorial policies. Jerome, despite his frustration with the unrelenting hostility of the *BG News*, defended the principle of freedom of the press; he urged legislators not to intervene, calling upon them to "have faith in your educational leaders—and particularly in your youth."

Much of the controversial content of the *BG News* dealt with its outspoken criticism of the Vietnam War. It divided Americans more deeply than any war in history, and nowhere were those divisions more evident than on the nation's campuses. As Roberta Libb Royhab, class of 1967, recalled: "we were all affected by the war, some in more tragic ways than others," At Bowling Green, discussions and "teach-ins" began as early as the spring of 1965 when President Lyndon Johnson was sending the first combat troops to Vietnam. During the next two years, a steadily increasing number of Americans of all ages questioned the indecisive war's necessity and morality, while others defended its purpose. Many students joined local chapters of the conservative Young Americans for Freedom and the liberal Students for a Democratic Society.

As on other campuses, the tempo of protest at Bowling Green increased, with the Williams Hall portico becoming the usual platform for speakers addressing crowds gathered on the lawn in front of University Hall and Moseley Hall. One of the largest protests was a part of a national "Day of Dissent" in October 1967, which attracted nearly 1,000 students to that site. Over the next several months, a number of prominent anti-

More than 7,000 people–students, faculty and townspeople– participated in an emotional candlelight march in response to the Kent State shootings in 1970.

war activists spoke on campus, while University student and faculty anti-war groups protested at the annual ROTC Review and sponsored silent vigils, a Draft Week and other programs. A petition to abolish the ROTC programs, with some 200 signatures, was published in the *BG News*. When national anti-war groups proclaimed a Vietnam Moratorium for Wednesday, Oct. 15, 1969, the Student Council and *BG News* called for students to show their support by boycotting classes. Some 3,500 students signed a telegram addressed to President Richard Nixon that called for the immediate withdrawal of U.S. troops from Vietnam. Students marched in a mock funeral procession from the University Union to the Bowling Green City Hall, and then returned for an afternoon "teach-in" on the steps of William Hall; the last speaker, urging moderation while sympathizing with the moratorium's goal, was Jerome. As some of the students formed a motorcade to Toledo to mail the telegram to the White House, others remained on campus for a "folk protest sing-in" in the Union oval.

The most intense moment came when President Nixon ordered U.S. troops to invade Cambodia on April 30, 1970. Protest erupted across the country, taking on increasingly confrontational overtones at many campuses, including at Kent State where Governor Rhodes ordered national guardsmen to the campus after the ROTC building was burned. On Monday, May 4, national guardsmen shot and killed four young people at Kent State. That afternoon hurriedly produced dittoed sheets, stating simply "Four Students Killed At Kent State," spread across campus. As on other campuses, the killing of students aroused indignation, shock and grief.

The next day a memorial service attended by students, faculty and staff closed with a promise to avoid violence on campus. Later that afternoon a special Faculty Senate meeting, with some 2,000 students and faculty in attendance, voted to cancel classes on Wednesday to honor the Kent State dead. A large gathering that day on the mall in front of Williams Hall–which Jerome later described as "the turning point in terms of … putting things into a constructive vein"–resulted in plans for a candlelight march through downtown Bowling Green that evening; 7,000-8,000 people, including hundreds of townspeople, joined in the emotional march.

At a time when many colleges were closing for the remainder of the spring term, the Faculty Senate held a special session on Sunday, May 10 to consider academic options which would enable the University to remain open; after much debate, it agreed to allow students to convert grades in any of their courses to a S-U basis and it authorized the establishment of special courses under what was called the New University (New U). More than 100 New U courses, all dealing in some way with contemporary issues, were quickly established, with enrollments ranging from a handful of students to more than 50. Altogether nearly 3,500 students participated in the New U.

Bowling Green was the only residential state university in Ohio not to close for some period during May 1970. Much of the credit was given to Jerome whose leadership, in the judgment of many observers, reflected firmness, openness and flexibility in both public forums and private planning meetings. Jerome cultivated and benefited from a student leadership that shared his determination to avoid confrontation. The compromises made to keep the University open triggered criticism, to be sure, as some faculty, students and parents disparaged the New U and S-U grades as, in the words of one parent who wrote to Jerome, "compromising with radicals and troublemakers."

The unprecedented turmoil occurred during Jerome's last year as president. The previous fall he had announced his resignation effective with the appointment of his successor. Jerome's decision to resign surprised many on campus. Privately, he offered two reasons, the first having to do with the optimum time for accomplishment: "I always had the theory that seven to 10 years was about the maximum you would have to put with a president in a growing institution. Secondly, he was discouraged by signs of greater control and fewer funds from Columbus:

" *I saw a change in the whole climate. I was in a growth climate. I saw the legislatures reacting to the outburst of the late 1960s with the student uprisings and so on. I knew they were going to limit the amount of money for education. So, I would have to go from a style which was really dream oriented … I thought there would have to be constraints, there would have to be some constrictions on this growth. That would call for a style that I was not ready to adjust to.* "

In the opinion of a number of faculty, staff and students, Jerome's finest hour as president was in responding to the unrest of May 1970. That may be true, but his leadership at that time ought not obscure seven years of articulating—frequently with eloquence—his vision for the University, fostering a genuinely collegial atmosphere and modifying the administrative structure to address new problems. While he was by no means a "quiet" leader, his self-confidence permitted him to deflect or share credit for accomplishments; he did not insist on being in the limelight. Hence faculty who saw him not accomplishing much may have appreciated only a part of an impressive record of building academic programs and fulfilling "dreams."

Indeed probably no other president enjoyed a greater degree of faculty confidence. Jerome's stature as an academic in his own right facilitated his interaction with faculty. Understanding the faculty's determination to play an enlarged role in governance, Jerome cultivated a working relationship with its leaders and helped to assure a firm foundation for the Faculty Senate. Jerome's cultivation of collegiality led to warm praise as his presidency ended. A Faculty Senate resolution singled out his role in strengthening the university community: "It is for the quality of life which he has brought to Bowling Green that we owe him our greatest debt. Although we cannot measure this quality, we can, and hereby do, affirm it."

In the middle of that tense month of May 1970, the Board of Trustees announced the appointment of Hollis A. Moore as the University's seventh president. The vice president for academic affairs at George Peabody College, a

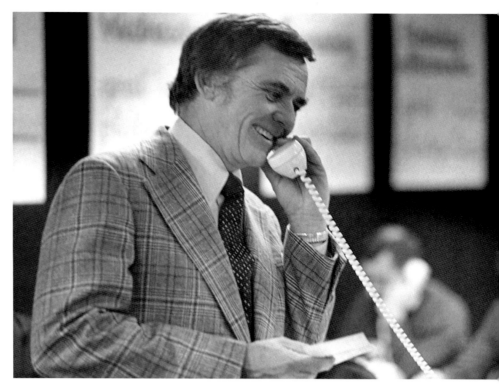

school best known for the training of teachers, the 47-year-old Moore held a doctorate in educational administration from the University of Texas and brought broad experience in higher education in the public and private sectors. Prior to going to George Peabody, he had served as executive secretary of the Committee for the Advancement of School Administration, director of education at the W. K. Kellogg Foundation and dean of education at the University of Arizona.

Moore had a strong interest in history, in which he had majored as a Baylor University undergraduate. He had a greater sense of institutional history than any Bowling Green president; he kept in his office artifacts from each of his predecessors and, well in advance of the University's 75th anniversary, he commissioned Stuart Givens of the history department to update the institution's official history for that occasion. He also studied closely, and was inspired by, the life and leadership of Woodrow Wilson; his widow Marian Moore recalled, "He never made a speech without quoting Woodrow Wilson."

The most persistent problem that Moore faced was clear by the time that he took office: support for higher education had leveled off. State funding had increased by nearly 40 percent during Jerome's administration, but the next decade brought unreliable support, marked by occasional cuts (the overall increase in subsidies

Hollis A Moore, the University's seventh president, worked for "a decade of distinction."

failing to keep pace with inflation) and, as a consequence, shifting more of the cost on to students (instructional fees income more than doubling from $8 million in 1970-71 to $17.3 million in 1980-81). The mood of the 1970s was reflected in Moore's decision to eschew an inauguration on the scale of those of McDonald and Jerome and to substitute a low-keyed and inexpensive President's Convocation, which was held in the spring of 1971. In his address on that occasion, Moore stated, "I have come to Bowling Green to work for this University because I genuinely believe that there can be ahead for us a decade of distinction like none of the six previous decades in the history of the institution." The "decade of distinction" was defined by the political and financial context. He recognized that the University would be caught between the demands of the state and some groups on campus for greater emphasis on the "practicality" of undergraduate education and the traditional liberal mission of a university. Indeed, much of his tenure would be engaged in trying to balance these different expectations at a time of financial restraint. Moore defined the task that he faced:

❝ During the 'golden years' leadership was seen as mediating conflicts between ambitious campus departments. During the recent period of campus disturbances, leadership was identified with keeping the peace. Now, in contrast to that recent past, leadership will be identified in the context of educational policymaking and resource planning. On campus and off it will be identified through the choices it makes. ❞

President Moore was a frequent guest at student organizations as part of his commitment to building a strong campus community.

To make the 1970s the "decade of distinction" meant less a vision of dramatic change than a commitment to marshalling resources to assure that University programs were of high quality. Moore once told a group, "What we do, we must do as well as we can." He was especially concerned about the quality of undergraduate education, leading him to promote change in the general education program. He supported other programmatic changes, most of which were generated "bottom-up"–which he correctly saw as evidence of faculty vitality–or had been in the planning stages as he took office. Finally, the "decade of distinction" reflected Moore's enormous pride in the University. He spent much time with students and faculty, engaged in what 20 years later would be termed "building community."

As much as he might have preferred otherwise, Moore devoted much time in his early months to "keeping the peace." The policies of Richard Nixon had a polarizing effect that was felt on college campuses. During Moore's first fall on campus, overflow audiences attended speeches by the "Chicago Seven" lawyer William Kunstler, who denounced the Nixon administration for suppressing dissent, and the antiwar actress Jane Fonda, who called for U.S. withdrawal from Vietnam and peaceful revolution at home. The following spring, a group of students calling themselves "Concerned People of BGSU," issued Moore a series of demands, including that he denounce the war in Vietnam, ban military recruitment on campus and prohibit campus police from carrying arms. Moore ignored the statement, but it was soon followed by a more insistent demand: the removal of ROTC from campus by ending academic credit for ROTC courses; this was strongly supported by the *BG News*. In May 1971, anti-ROTC demonstrators marched to Memorial Hall, which housed the ROTC programs, and protested the annual ROTC review, which was held in the area behind Memorial Hall. When a number of protesters surged through the roped-off area and spilled out on the field, Moore cancelled the review. Afterward, demonstrators resumed a vigil outside Memorial Hall, which prompted a return visit by Kunstler who said, "What you do here … one tiny demonstration, is as significant as anything else in the world." The protest was defused when the Academic Council referred the academic credit issue to the College of Business Administration, which housed the ROTC programs. When the granting ROTC credit was upheld, the *BG News* editorialized: "We would like to commend the College of Business Curriculum Committee for completely living up to our expectations."

While dealing with the ferment on campus, Moore fashioned his administration. Like other presidents, Moore reorganized the administrative structure, most notably by enhancing the authority of provost (and dropping the designation of vice president for academic affairs from the title), with vice provosts for faculty affairs, student affairs, research and graduate studies and continuing education. He also established the position of vice president of resource planning (originally coordinator for planning and budgeting). In revamping the administration, Moore was hampered by the presence of three "Jerome men" as vice presidents—Stanley Coffman, B. D. Owens, James Bond—each of whom had presidential ambitions and one of whom (Bond) had been a finalist for the University presidency in 1970. Most problematic was Coffman; like other presidents, Moore considered appointment of the chief academic officer to be his most important prerogative; as described by one confidante, he "loathed the situation" that he inherited. It was not until 1972 that Coffman resigned to become president of the State University of New York College at New Paltz (by that time Owens and Bond had also left to become the presidents of the University of Tampa and California State College at Sacramento, respectively). Following a year's search for a provost, Moore was three years into his presidency before he was finally able to appoint his chief academic officer.

To fill the two new positions of provost and vice president of resource planning, Moore took pride in calling upon relatively young and inexperienced men whom he considered especially talented—in Moore's words, "appointing a 32-year-old 'wave-maker' from Penn as provost" and "establishing resource planning under a 32-year-old management expert." Kenneth Rothe, a physicist who had been assistant dean of arts and sciences at the University of Pennsylvania, became provost in 1973, joining Michael J. Ferrari, who had been chairman of the management department at Kent State University when Moore had named him vice president of resource planning in 1971. Moore actually hired a third 32-year-old when he recruited Richard Edwards in 1971 from the director's office of the National Science Foundation to become executive assistant to the president. With the retirement of Kenneth McFall in 1975, Edwards replaced him as vice president and secretary to the Board of Trustees. To administer non-academic areas, Moore also established the position of vice president for operations.

... Moore sought "to make Bowling Green ... something very distinctive, a very special place. He talked about a decade of distinction ... and I think he really meant it."

Moore brought to the presidency a deliberative and low-keyed approach, one that relied heavily on subordinates. Ferrari described him "as an idea person, [who] was also a tremendous 'delegator'—throw out to the vice presidents and let them run with it." Dean Karl Vogt put it bluntly: Moore was "great for the College of Business Administration because he didn't do a whole hell of a lot. He just let you do your own thing. He didn't encourage or discourage." This approach avoided confrontations; Ferrari recalled, "You rarely found Hollis Moore engaged in a sharp conflict environment, he would never be in it." So Moore, who maintained a formal style, kept a certain distance from those in his inner circle, expecting them to fulfill his expectations but rarely commenting on their work.

The low-key style belied Moore's determination to give Bowling Green a "touch of class" physically and academically. Moore loved BGSU and he was totally passionate about all facets of the University.

He cared a lot about the physical appearance of the campus and did an annual tour of the campus in a golf cart with the vice president for finance and administration and his staff. He inspected the campus with a 'fine-toothed comb.' Clearly, everyone had his or her 'marching orders' on what needed to be done before the opening of the new school year.

From Branch Campuses to Firelands

During the 1950s, the University renewed its commitment to off-campus instruction. Extension courses had been interrupted by World War II and were difficult to resume during the postwar period because of the teacher shortage, but as main campus enrollments stabilized, the University established four branches that were destined to serve hundreds of residents throughout northwest Ohio. A branch at Sandusky was reopened in 1956-57 (the initial effort to develop a branch there a decade earlier had been abandoned), and branches at Bryan, Fremont and Fostoria followed over the next three years. (A branch was also established at Mansfield in 1954-55, but it was transferred to Oho State four years later.) The branches offered late afternoon and evening instruction in local high schools, were taught mostly by regular University faculty, and enabled students to complete general education requirements at the branches. According to the *BGSU Branch News*, published by the Office of Summer and Off-Campus Programs, a branch system of student government, as well as social events at the branches and access to athletic and other events on the main campus, cultivated a sense of "identity" and "belonging" to the University. By the 1960s, about 1,000 students were enrolled each semester in branch (now designated "academic centers") courses. By the late 1960s, enrollments began to decline and within a few years, the branches were closed. This resulted from the growth of the state's commitment to establishing two-year community colleges and a declining main campus commitment at a time when new programs were being developed and faculty resources were increasingly needed on campus.

The demise of the branches, however, paralleled the emergence of a distinctive and enduring campus at Huron. This development reflected the ties between Bowling Green and the Huron-Sandusky area. Sandusky always attracted the largest enrollments of branch students. In 1949, the University's theatre program had established its still-running summer playhouse at Huron. In the mid-1960s, a number of civic leaders in Erie, Huron and Ottawa counties began working for a permanent campus that would offer the first two years of academic programs with courses in the day and evening. Led by Theodore Wakefield of Huron, a successful fundraising campaign convinced OBOR to support the project. In the fall of 1968, the Firelands Campus opened, with its $3 million building and 30 faculty members. Appropriately, one of the last issues of *The Center News* featured a former Sandusky student who was anticipating the move to Firelands Campus as "quite an improvement."

The Huron-Sandusky communities worked diligently to establish BGSU Firelands in the late 1960s.

On the academic side, according to Ferrari, Moore sought "to make Bowling Green … something very distinctive, a very special place. He talked about a decade of distinction … and I think he really meant it." Moore's concern with undergraduate education was a timely priority. He seized upon a report, "The Mission of the University," prepared by Academic Council in the spring of 1970, which called for more innovative approaches to teaching and for a broad-based, liberal education for all students. Student unrest, the report suggested, was based partly on criticism of the traditional curriculum and instructional methods, especially reliance on large lecture sections in lower division courses.

In his first year in office, Moore appointed a "Blue Ribbon" Committee on general education, which recommended reconsideration of the curriculum that would provide training in areas to "serve society's future needs" which included health and social services, environmental control, industrial technology and recreation. At the same time, the Academic Council established the Academic Development and Evaluation Committee System, which endorsed efforts to stimulate pedagogical reform and won warm praise from Moore for providing "the mechanism for allowing the university to function in a state of perpetual transformation."

In the spirit of these calls for reform, the University launched a host of programs with the primary objective to improve general education. Besides the New U, which resumed with limited courses, in 1970-71 the Honors Program was replaced by the Experimental Studies Program, which emphasized individual instruction. The Little College—intended to promote interdisciplinary learning with an emphasis on fostering critical thinking and individual values—began with 90 students and four faculty engaged in a course, "The Making and Manipulation of Images." The more intensive Cluster Colleges initiative was launched in 1971-72; these were one-quarter "living-learning" experiences focusing on the humanities and physical sciences. A $142,000 grant from the Carnegie Foundation in 1972 supported the development of a Modular Achievement Program (MAP), which was to offer an integrated program of study to facilitate a more efficient means of completing general education requirements.

Two years later, thanks to the promise of MAP, a $500,000 grant from the Fund for the Improvement of Postsecondary Education supported the founding of the Competency-based Undergraduate Education (CUE) Center, to study and to enhance the essential skills and capabilities associated with general education. The premise of these initiatives was that interdisciplinary, discussion-based and relatively small classes would enhance general education. While many faculty enthusiastically endorsed and participated in the programs, others questioned their effectiveness. An evaluation of the Little College, for instance, found that course content was sacrificed in the interest of "self-realization and understanding." The emphasis on "relevancy" in some of the initiatives troubled defenders of the traditional liberal education; 30 members of the psychology department, issued a position paper criticizing the "job-training" and calling for recognition of a university's "devotion to excellence in the creation, examination and dissemination of knowledge."

Rothe, upon taking over as provost in 1973, supported these curricular initiatives and pressed academic departments to support them. To assure coordination and evaluation, the Academic Council, at Rothe's urging, approved the establishment of the University Division of General Studies with responsibility for administering general education courses, coordinating interdisciplinary and experimental courses, and formulating a statement of general education goals and skills.

The various initiatives and their supportive administrative structure yielded modest results. Evaluating curricular reform is difficult. Perhaps the greatest impact of the innovation was in calling attention to some widely held criticisms of general education, showing the potential of the experimental programs and in clarifying the objectives of general education. The initiatives affected a minority of students; most undergraduate instruction in 1980 resembled that of 1970—relatively large, discipline-based lecture classes. Moore's support of innovations such as the Little College and Cluster College demonstrated a pragmatism that the situation demanded, but he and the provost did not press for early systematic evaluations of such experiments, which might have addressed concerns of critics and won greater faculty support. A provost with greater academic

stature and more experience than Rothe would have carried more authority in pressing for reform and in gaining faculty support. Rothe, to his credit, was never an uncritical supporter of innovation. In his final report before leaving office in 1978, he stated:

> *" Even a modicum of honesty requires us to admit that neither our general education program nor the majority of such programs nationally has succeeded in producing the breadth of knowledge or honing of the intellect, let alone the lesser skills attained such as reading, writing and basic mathematics. "*

By the time Moore had a provost who enjoyed his full confidence and wide respect on campus—when Ferrari replaced Rothe in 1978—he was already eight years into his presidency and the University was beset by financial constraints, which make non-traditional academic units especially vulnerable. "Top-down" curricular innovation without strong connections to traditional departments is always difficult to sustain. For various reasons, Moore's successors established other priorities.

Although the general education reform seemed his priority, Moore supported other initiatives, which reflected his assumption that "distinction" depended on enhancing quality while promoting limited and manageable changes. True to Moore's administrative style, much change was from the "bottom up," but he actively supported and, at times, championed initiatives.

Responding to a changing job market and the Blue Ribbon Committee's call for training to meet "society's future needs," the University in 1973 established the College of Health and Community Services, the first new college in 38 years. Intended to train technical specialists in the expanding health and social services fields, the college expanded in the next few years with the addition of programs in nursing and communication disorders, which were transferred from the College of Arts and Sciences.

The College of Musical Arts was established in 1975, elevating its status from school (in the College of Education) to college. The change recognized the stature of its performing faculty and program, which was further enhanced by construction of the Musical Arts Center, which was completed in 1979. Hollis and Marian

Moore took a strong interest in the arts and played a prominent role in raising funds for the performance areas: the Lenore and Marvin Kobacker Hall and the Dorothy and Ashel Bryan Recital Hall. This led the Board of Trustees later to rename the building the Hollis and Marian Moore Musical Arts Center, noting, "Dr. Moore, almost single-handedly, was responsible for the planning and fundraising which made the facility a reality."

At the graduate level, four new doctoral programs—in history, mathematics and statistics, sociology and the interdisciplinary American culture studies—were established at a time of increasingly rigorous OBOR review. Moore and Charles Leone, who was vice provost for research and dean of the Graduate College, worked diligently to secure OBOR approval. This brought the number of programs to nine, with little expectation of further development at that level, as the Board of Regents issued a virtual moratorium on doctoral programs.

At the undergraduate level, the call of student activists, supported by many faculty, for attention to the study of African-Americans, Hispanics, and other minorities as well as of women led to the launching of courses in Afro-American, Latino and women's studies. By 1979 under the leadership of Robert Perry, the interdisciplinary ethnic studies program evolved into the ethnic studies department.

Paralleling that development, Dean John Ericksen of the College of Arts and Sciences in 1975 asked Susan Arpad, who had just joined the popular culture department, whether Bowling Green needed a women's studies program. A committee, chaired by Arpad, promptly replied in the affirmative and two years later it fashioned an interdisciplinary curriculum, which was approved by OBOR and became Ohio's first undergraduate degree program in women's studies.

The women's studies program drew upon the emergence of faculty women as a political force seeking to address inequality and to play a more prominent role in University affairs. In 1972 the Women's Equity Action League (WEAL) filed a complaint with the Department of Health, Education and Welfare charging that the University discriminated against women as a class in admissions, financial aid, hiring, tenure, promotion and salary. That action grew out of a Faculty Senate ad hoc Committee on the Status

In 1973, the University established the College of Health and Community Services—the first new college in 38 years.

of Women, which following a year of study, found "substantial evidence" of discrimination against female faculty members; the Faculty Senate endorsed the committee's recommendations for measures to address any abuses. Not until 1978 did the Office of Civil Rights complete its investigation of the WEAL complaint and conclude, "It did not find that a preponderance of evidence indicated that women are discriminated against." By that time Moore had addressed some of the concerns by establishing an Office of Equal Opportunity and developing an Affirmative Action Program. Also, in 1973 the University abandoned its clearly discriminatory "gender-balanced" admissions policy, which subjected women applicants to an early "closing" date. The implementation of a "sex-blind" admission policy ended the days of a 50-50 gender division in the undergraduate student body (men usually slightly outnumbered women) and brought an era of predominantly female undergraduate students (58 percent by 1980).

Significant in advancing women's interest was the Women's Caucus, an informal group of 20-25 faculty, which grew out of the salary study of 1971-72. Prominent among its leaders were Janis L. Pallister (romance languages), Greer Litton Fox (sociology), Rena Foy (education), Jaffran Jones (music) and Ramona Cormier (philosophy), who chaired the group from 1975-78. Besides "awakening" other women to discrimination and mentoring younger faculty, the Women's Caucus also sought, with considerable success, to promote female representation on University committees and in administrative positions. In 1978, Ferrari named Cormier to the position of associate provost—the highest-ranking position held by a woman to that time. Five years later with the appointment of two female vice-presidents, the Women's Caucus considered its objectives substantially achieved.

A quiet, but significant, initiative on behalf of "distinction" was Moore's unequivocal support for bringing a Phi Beta Kappa chapter to Bowling Green. The nation's oldest and most prestigious academic honorary society had a rigorous review process for new chapters. Stuart Givens of the history faculty, with Moore's backing, began the arduous application process, which led ultimately to the awarding of a chapter in 1982.

Complementing his support of academic initiatives, Moore excelled at the less formal, but equally vital, presidential responsibilities. On the "public relations" side, he built on the development programs established by his predecessor and also cultivated support from alumni and the Toledo business and professional community. Annual alumni giving increased substantially: from $89,000 in 1970 to more than $500,000 by 1980. Moore was also conscious of the importance of faculty support; as Marian Moore recalled, "He always said that you get your job from the Board of Trustees, whether you kept it depends on the support of faculty." Through his relationship with the Faculty Senate and his presence at less-formal faculty gatherings, Moore cultivated the support and respect of the faculty. He took pride in faculty accomplishments, often writing notes of congratulation. When the first Distinguished University Professor, Eugene Lukacs, mathematics, was named in 1974, Moore made certain that its significance was appropriately recognized. He established the practice of a University-wide convocation, with the president presiding, where the title was conferred and the honoree presented a lecture. During his presidency, five other outstanding faculty were named Distinguished University Professor: Frank Baldanza, English (1974); Ray B. Browne, popular culture (1977); Janis L. Pallister, romance languages (1979); Bernard Sternsher, history (1979), and William B. Jackson, biological sciences (1981).

Where Moore truly excelled was in his relationship with students. He was, with the exception of Prout, the University's most "visible" president. The Moores were student-oriented, opening the president's home to students with problems, hosting many student groups and beginning the tradition of the senior picnic. Together with his wife Marian, he was a fixture at athletic events, fraternity and sorority parties, plays, concerts and various other gatherings. Richard Eakin, who joined the mathematics faculty in 1965 and became vice provost for student affairs during Moore's presidency, recalled, "He was fairly formal, but he was more than wiling to be available to [students] for social events. He followed an incredible social schedule. I often thought too much, but maybe you can't do that too much. He would just really go to great lengths to go to fraternity parties, Panhellic desserts, almost anything you could name in terms of student functions … he did so with great social style." Richard Edwards added, "When in town, he wouldn't think of missing a BGSU hockey game and bringing many friends. He and Mrs. Moore were everywhere about the campus."

Moore was also passionate about engaging students in the governance system and worked closely with student leaders.

When Moore attended athletic events, it was not to be seen, but to cheer Bowling Green to victory. He loved to win, and he took defeat hard. Unfortunately, the 1970s was not especially auspicious for the traditional major sports—men's basketball and football—but the newly established hockey program achieved national prominence. Under coach Ron Mason, the Falcons were one of the dominant teams in the Central College Hockey Association and made the NCAA play-offs three times. Two Bowling Green players—Ken Morrow and Mark Wells—played on the legendary 1980 U.S. Olympic team, which won the gold medal. Besides hockey, the track team was remarkably successful. Otherwise, "competitive but not championship" teams prevailed. The basketball team won its last outright MAC title (and made its last NCAA appearance) in 1967-

The Long Tradition of Women's Sports[1]

Field hockey was one of the women's teams that flourished during the 1970s.

As the second half of the twentieth century dawned, the BGSU women's sports program was flourishing as a student-centered enterprise administered through the intramural program in Women's Health and Physical Education. Dorothy Luedtke, who had been appointed advisor of the Women's Recreation Association in 1948, led the development of the sports program as director of women's intramurals from 1955 to 1968.

During the 1950s, existing clubs continued to excel, and several new clubs were formed. As 1955 Novice National AAU champions and winners of the Annual Intercollegiate Meet in 1957 and 1959, the Swan Club dominated intercollegiate synchronized swimming for much of this decade. Volleyball and softball competition began in 1956.

By 1961, BGSU boasted fifteen15 women's sports clubs in addition to coeducational volleyball, bowling, tennis and badminton. It was becoming apparent that many of these clubs were actually varsity teams participating in intercollegiate competition. The first intercollegiate basketball competition took place during the 1962-63 academic year with teams from Adrian College, Kent State University, University of Dayton and University of Michigan. In 1965 a gymnastics club was created, and fast-pitch softball acquired club status.

During the 1970s, women's sports continued to prosper, fielding teams in basketball, cross country, fencing, field hockey, golf, gymnastics, lacrosse, swimming, synchronized swimming, tennis, track and volleyball, and operating under the auspices of the Association for Intercollegiate Athletics for Women (AIAW). Title IX was passed in 1972, and in 1976 the BGSU women's and men's varsity athletics programs merged. President Hollis Moore tapped Sue Hager, who had been director of women's intramurals since 1968, as acting associate athletic director in charge of nonrevenue sports. In the fall of 1976, Carole Huston was named associate athletic director and was the first woman in the U.S. to be appointed as a full-time administrator of NCAA Division I women's and men's nonrevenue sports. The women's teams continued to compete under the aegis of the AIAW until 1982, when the NCAA initiated championships in D-I women's sports, and the AIAW ceased to exist. Since then, women's athletics at BGSU has continued its longstanding tradition of excellence.

> Janet Parks and Ann Bowers

---

1. A more complete history of BGSU women's sports can be found in *Forward Falcons: Women's Sports at Bowling Green State University, 1914-1982* (www.lulu.com).

68. Football, which was Moore's greatest passion, had winning records, but no MAC titles and frustrating defeats at the hands of Miami. After a third straight setback in 1976, Moore forced the resignation of head coach Don Nehlen, despite an 8-3 season. That action led some on the faculty and local sportswriters to question Moore's priorities. Similar questions were raised when he recruited a high-powered athletic director from UCLA, who resigned after a few weeks—perhaps Moore's most embarrassing episode.

Moore was also passionate about engaging students in the governance system and worked closely with student leaders. William Arnold, class of 1974 who was student body president recalled:

" What a great president Hollis Moore was. I did a lot of work with him in those days. He was especially good at listening to the students' views … He was always willing to listen. He took the time and I always remembered that. I don't think you can lead well unless you are a good listener. "

Moore took advantage of what the departing Jerome in 1970 considered the most important "unfinished business " of his administration: a broadly based community council with considerable student representation to deal with all aspects of university policy. After nearly three years of continuing discussion, Moore in 1973 appointed a Committee on University Governance and Reorganization, which two years later put forth its proposals that culminated in the adoption of the Academic Charter in 1976. By that time, much of the 1960s emotion surrounding student involvement in university governance had abated, but the Academic Charter formalized student representation in the Faculty Senate, recommended student representation on most university committees, but continued the duality of a student and faculty governing bodies.

This outcome disappointed many student leaders. Despite lengthy discussion, student government was in a state of uncertainty. Leaders faced the problem of student apathy, which has long plagued student government at most universities, but was aggravated by the students' interest in "careerism." The lack of interest also came from the widely held belief that SGA had few responsibilities and little power. Typically fewer than 10 percent of students voted in elections and a lack of candidates twice forced the delay of elections. The *BG News* asserted in 1977: "It is time to form a student government with real power and the ability to work together. Striving for anything less than that is simply inviting mediocrity." After four years of no progress and another deferral of elections, the *BG News* wrote: "Will there be an SGA? Does anyone care?" In sum, the shared governance that many had anticipated emerging from the turmoil of 1970 was never realized—much to the chagrin of both Jerome and Moore.

Student expectations and priorities changed significantly. "The steady state institution" of the 1970s brought a modest eight percent enrollment increase (1,500 students), while overall size of the faculty and staff remained stable. Resources had to be reallocated to meet changing interests and programs. The College of Education lost its position as the principal undergraduate college, with a nearly 50 percent reduction in its majors, a development driven in large part by female students increasingly entering nontraditional fields. Meanwhile, the College of Business Administration, which had long been the third-ranking college, emerged as the enrollment leader. The College of Arts and Sciences, which lost some students to the new College of Health and Community Services, remained the second-ranking college. The spectacular growth of Business Administration (its enrollment doubling to nearly 4,800 students during the decade) and the programs in the Health and Community Services (its enrollment reached nearly 1,400 by 1980) reflected the student demand for a more career-oriented, professional undergraduate education.

Moore's determined interest in meeting student needs and interests led him to support the construction of the Student Recreation Center (SRC), which opened in 1979—the first facility of its kind on any Ohio campus. This decision, which was controversial, came at a time of limited state support for capital expenditures. The movement for the SRC developed among students during the mid-1970s when the nation experienced a "fitness craze." Critics, which included some students and members of the Board of Trustees, contended that the "craze" would pass, leaving the University with a large, partially used building, and that the cost, in any event, would be passed along largely to students. Reports in the *BG News* voiced concern that a mandatory student fee to construct and

maintain a facility would benefit intercollegiate athletics, not the student body as a whole. That was never the SRC planners' intent and, in fact, the swimming teams were the only intercollegiate sport to use the SRC for practice and meets. With the strong support of Moore joined by student leaders, the Board of Trustees approved construction. Once opened, the SRC quickly became a widely used by students, faculty, staff and community (non-students were required to pay for memberships) and became one of the University's "selling points" to prospective students.

Although Moore generally enjoyed a cordial relationship with the faculty, he faced a strong movement for collective bargaining—the result of discontent generated by evidence that faculty salaries were failing to keep pace with inflation and were falling behind those at other universities. Sensitive to criticism of the salary structure, Moore and the Board of Trustees had attempted to blunt it in 1975 by instituting a Special Achievement Award Program, which provided $1,000 "bonuses" as supplemental pay to selected faculty for outstanding research, teaching and service. This initiative won Moore few friends, because the selection process generated controversy. After

Students were at the heart of the decision to build the Student Recreation Center in the late 1970s.

Michael "Mick" Ferrari served as interim president after Hollis Moore's death and was the campus choice for his replacement.

two years, Moore abandoned the program. By 1978, Moore accepted the necessity of authorizing a collective bargaining election, which was scheduled for January 1979. Although he avoided involvement in the debate, Moore privately considered collective bargaining to be "undemocratic" and was apprehensive that a majority of faculty would vote for it. The election, expected to be close, resulted in the faculty voting down collective bargaining, 311 in favor and 320 opposed.

Within the next year, the University community became increasingly aware of Moore's recurring health problems, which were attributed to myelofibrosis. By late 1980 those who worked closest with him noticed that had become more distant and aloof. His condition then suddenly worsened, and in February 1981 he entered the Medical College of Ohio Hospital in Toledo for treatment of a "low malignancy" brain tumor. On April 19, he died. A large campus memorial service witnessed an emotional outpouring of sympathy for Marian Moore and grief over the loss of a respected leader. In a resolution, the Faculty Senate appropriately praised "his moral integrity, his creativity, his sense of style, his flair for living, his lively intellectual curiosity and his friendly manner ..." In an editorial Toledo television anchor, Frank Venner, said: "Dr. Moore stressed excellence in every function of the university. He was not afraid of change or new ideas. ... His touch of class was something special."

Called upon to lead the University during a difficult decade, Moore demonstrated both a timely vision and generally sound political instincts. His emphasis on lower division undergraduate curriculum and instruction was entirely justified. To achieve his academic priorities, Moore needed a strong provost in any event, but especially so in his case because of, as Ferrari put it, "his reluctance to be assertive. I thought he had built the base to make it happen, but he didn't." So in terms of his principal goal, the pity may be that the curricular momentum of the Moore years was not pressed vigorously at the opportune time only to lose priority in the following decade.

That being said, the University benefited from the steady leadership, the integrity and the dedication of Hollis Moore. Despite the constraints of the "steady state," Bowling Green did experience, in many ways, a "decade of distinction."

After Moore's death, the Board of Trustees named Ferrari as interim president and Edwards as executive vice president. It also established an 18-person Presidential Search and Screening Committee, composed, as that of 1970, of Board members, administrators, faculty, students and alumni. From the beginning, the committee was controversial. In the fall of 1981, the Faculty Senate called for an open search, objecting in particular to a statement by Frazier Reams Jr., the chairman of the Board of Trustees and of the Search Committee, which indicated that the search would be conducted in secrecy and that nothing more would be said publicly until the search was completed. To many on the faculty and staff, it seemed that the determined secrecy was intended to silence any campus support for Ferrari, who was known to be a candidate. Moreover, in the previous decade, searches for academic positions had become more open; the days of "old boys' networks" had yielded to affirmative action and equal opportunity procedures. The Board of Trustees ignored the Faculty Senate's concerns.

The Search and Screening Committee proceeded. It seriously considered approximately 30 candidates out of nearly 150 applicants and nominees, before narrowing the field to 10. Teams of three or more committee members interviewed each of the candidates and reported back to the full committee, which then determined the five finalists. This meant the entire committee did not meet all of the finalists prior to their being selected. On Feb. 11, 1982 the committee submitted its five finalists, with Ferrari's name among them. During the first week of March, each of the five finalists was interviewed by the full Board of Trustees and given a tour of the campus and the president's residence. This was notably more "secretive" than the two previous searches in which finalists had met selected groups when they visited campus. In the end, a majority of the board, led by Reams, favored changing the direction of the University, which assured an external selection. On March 15, 1982, Reams announced the appointment of Paul J. Olscamp as the University's eighth president.

Dave Wottle: Olympic Champion

The track team, under coach Mel Brodt, achieved its greatest success with two long-distance runners achieving national renown: Sid Sink and Dave Wottle. The 1972 yearbook, featuring an article on Sink and Wottle, concluded "their outstanding efforts have brought track fame to Bowling Green. Their next goal is to bring fame to the United States in the 1972 Olympics." It was Wottle who brought that fame by winning the 800-meter run in the games held that summer in Munich. Wottle had graduated from Bowling Green in June of 1972 and gotten married prior to the Olympics. On Sept. 2, Wottle came from back in the field during the final lap, and in a photo finish narrowly edged the Soviet runner Yevgeny Arzhanov by three hundredths of a second. Wottle recalled: "I didn't know if I had won. I just knew I was close. It took them five minutes to determine who won. That seemed like an eternity." Finally, his name flashed on the scoreboard as the winner. Wottle's victory is best remembered for the iconic photograph as "the slender man with a golf cap" standing on the winner's stand, hand over heart, as the national anthem was played. In the excitement of victory, who could fault him for wearing the cap?

Olscamp, who was completing his seventh year as president of Western Washington University, was the first president to come from a liberal arts background and also had an impressive scholarly record. A native of Canada, he earned bachelor's and master's degrees at the University of Western Ontario and a doctorate in philosophy at the University of Rochester. Prior to going to Western Washington, he had served as vice president for academic affairs at Roosevelt University in Chicago.

The appointment triggered controversy. Few critics questioned Olscamp's qualifications, instead focusing on the search process and the rejection of Ferrari, who enjoyed considerable support among faculty, staff and townspeople. Although never acknowledged, Ferrari's popularity influenced the secrecy of the search. That apprehension was unfair to faculty and others who would have been interviewing finalists for the position, for it assumed that they were incapable of making fair assessments of candidates and to consider the strengths/weaknesses of all of them, including Ferrari. The *Bowling Green Daily Sentinel-Tribune*, which rarely takes editorial positions, strongly criticized the Board of Trustees and called upon readers to engage in a massive letter writing campaign to members of the board, urging that they reconsider the appointment before it was made official at the board's April 9 meeting. On April 6, about one-half of the faculty answered the summons of senate leaders for a general meeting, which resulted in the passage of two resolutions: the first congratulated Olscamp on his appointment and thanked Ferrari for his service; the second indicted the Board of Trustees for its "growing disposition to act unilaterally and in isolation" which had led to a "dramatic erosion of mutual trust and respect" between the board and faculty.

Despite the strident criticism of the Board, most faculty were not prepared to join in the *Sentinel-Tribune* call for the board to reverse its decision—an action which would have alienated relations with Olscamp, whose appointment, all recognized, was inevitable. The Undergraduate Student Government passed a set of resolutions similar to those of the faculty. The resolutions were presented at the Board of Trustees meeting on April 9, when the Olscamp appointment was formalized.

Whatever the reasons for the board's decision, it treated Ferrari rather shabbily, not telling him when it had decided on an external candidate ("there was little eye contact with me … I knew it was over") until a few days before it was announced and not expressing appreciation for his service. Ferrari remained at Bowling Green in 1982-83 as Trustee Professor of Administration, before leaving to become provost at Wright State University; he later was president of Drake University and Chancellor of Texas Christian University.

So the period between 1961 and 1982 was bracketed by controversies centering on the presidency: the faculty and student "rebellion" against McDonald; the faculty and student discontent with the Board's process in selecting a president and overlooking a popular internal candidate. Those divisive moments notwithstanding, the intervening two decades witnessed significant advancement by the "maturing university" that Jerome saw as he assumed the presidency. ■

1982-1995
A New Direction:
The Olscamp Presidency

The presidency of Paul J. Olscamp brought a period of accomplishment, principally through the enhanced national "visibility" of outstanding academic programs; it also witnessed considerable controversy resulting from criticism of his "new direction" for the University and of his leadership style.

Paul Olscamp became BGSU's eighth president in 1982.

Olscamp's difficulties also stemmed from the legacy of the controversy surrounding the presidential selection process in 1981-82. Thus, for much of his 13 years as president, Olscamp was a polarizing figure. To his admirers, Olscamp provided the University with a clear sense of direction, strengthened its academic programs and stature, allocated resources to support areas of excellence, established programs to attract outstanding undergraduate students, only to have his efforts persistently undermined by petty critics. To his detractors, Olscamp was insensitive to faculty opinion, manipulated the governance process and administrative appointments, built a few programs at the expense of others and undermined the University's traditional undergraduate mission.

When the Board of Trustees began its search in 1981, its advertised criteria for the president were typically bland, but the sense of the need for leadership that would provide a "new direction" took hold among a majority of its members. Olscamp later reflected:

❝ *[Frazier Reams] was the decisive person in saying, 'No, let's go outside the University, let's get somebody new, let's get somebody who's going to change the direction of this institution ... somebody who's just not going to be satisfied with what's always been true around here.'* ❞

The Board of Trustees left it to Olscamp to determine the "new direction." He chose the traditional path of enhancing a university's stature through respected programs built on faculty research. In addition, the state legislature's "ceiling" on enrollments at 15,000 full-time equivalent students (FTEs) made it expedient to increase the percentage of graduate students who brought higher subsidies; moreover, they provided teaching and research assistance. Four years into his presidency, Olscamp believed he was fulfilling that "new direction," seeing himself as a transforming figure:

    I think my appointment as president of this institution will turn out to have been one of the more important appointments made in its brief history, because of the nature of the things that have happened ... It will be very hard for another president to come in and get the university off this track.

Olscamp's claim in 1986 was a tribute to his early skill in gaining support for a "new direction" and implanting measures that changed the University. The situation that he encountered in 1982 was not auspicious. Although Olscamp correctly observed that the criticism surrounding the Board of Trustees' conduct of the search had nothing to do with his qualifications, controversy dogged his administration from the time of his appointment. When a condition of that appointment—that the Board assured a position for his wife, Ruth Olscamp, a speech pathologist who had been a clinic coordinator at Western Washington University—became known, many faculty were disturbed, especially in light of the financial problems at the University, which had led to a hiring freeze in 1981-82. She was appointed an assistant professor of communications disorders in the College of Health and Community Services. In late August 1982 Olscamp, who had assumed office on July 1, was not on campus for the annual Opening Day, when the President traditionally addresses the entire faculty. Many were annoyed by his absence (which had been approved by the Board of Trustees), especially because the financial crisis continued and his absence was for a long-planned sailing trip from Hawaii to the state of Washington.

On October 1, when Olscamp finally spoke to the faculty and staff in his first State of the University address, he outlined a number of initiatives including enhancing academic programs by strengthening the faculty, expanding academic-based scholarships and increasing funding for the library whose holdings were "not adequate for an institution of this size and scope." He was also forthright about the campus political situation: the "foundation of a successful university community ... [is] based upon trust, not upon affection for the leadership of the institution, nor upon tradition

alone, nor upon personal acquaintance or liking of individuals." He pledged that he would be candid, honest and open and would work to earn the respect of faculty, including those who disagreed with his priorities.

As this address suggested, Olcamp, more than any president with the possible exception of McDonald, began his term with a clearly defined agenda and a determination to achieve his objectives early in his administration. He came with "a full-fledged concept ... of how an institution ought to work from a planning and budgeting point of view" (an implicit criticism of Michael Ferrari's work) and to the centrality of a clear sense of direction and priorities. He later acknowledged that he probably "complain[ed] a little too much to too many people about the situation that existed when I first came to this school." He was indeed disappointed by much of what he inherited. Previous administrations, he thought, had failed to give sufficient attention to the securing of external fundraising, to recruiting minority students and national merit scholars, and to establishing another professional school. He was also dismayed by the lack of a mission statement. Lastly, he was appalled by the undergraduate curriculum especially the smorgasbord of general education courses, which permitted students to graduate "without taking a set of courses in the traditional liberal arts core." He said:

    If there were a single way that I was going to improve the undergraduate curriculum, it would be [to] make it impossible for anyone to graduate without taking a set of courses in the traditional liberal arts core; that's what I would do. I would want to be able to say to everybody in the country that it's not possible to graduate from Bowling Green and have taken no courses in comparative history, no course in philosophy, no course in literature, no course in a quantitative discipline, but I can't say that right now.

Olscamp's "take-charge" approach impressed a number of his subordinates. Richard Eakin, who was vice provost for student affairs when Olscamp took office, observed, "[Olscamp] has articulated more aspirations for Bowling Green than perhaps either [Jerome or Moore] ... He's not afraid to put some ideas on the table and find out how people respond to them ... He's going to challenge the university to do things."

The Changing Campus Scene

Amidst a number of major construction projects between 1982 and 1985, the most modest new building was the most widely used. A new Visitors Center was built to replace the previous "little green shack" that had been in place since 1975. The new facility, visible approaching campus from I-75 on East Wooster Street, had a drive-through that was manned by students.

In 1984 the Physical Sciences Building, a $7.2 million five-story facility, housing the chemistry department and the physics and astronomy department, opened. It featured a 188-seat planetarium and a rooftop observatory.

In 1992 the new Fine Arts Center was dedicated, which brought all five divisions of the School of Art under one roof. In addition to classrooms, studios and offices, it included the new Dorothy Uber Bryan and Hiroko Nakamoto galleries, which provided 7,000 square-feet to display student works and major art exhibitions. The Bryan Gallery, the largest exhibition area, was underwritten by a donation of $250,000 by Dorothy & Ashel Bryan. The adjacent Nakamoto Gallery was constructed under the supervision of Nakamoto, an internationally known interior designer and BGSU alumna; it features an authentic Japanese tea ceremony room to be used for formal tea ceremony instruction and other special purposes.

The arts on campus received a boost with the addition of the Hiroko Nakamoto (pictured above) and the Dorothy Uber Bryan galleries.

In 1994 Olscamp Hall was dedicated, which addressed the longstanding shortage of classroom space. This $13.5 million "state-of-the-art" building was one of most technologically advanced classroom settings in the state. The two-story, 95,000-square-foot building had the capacity to accommodate more than 2,000 students in 28 classrooms and lecture halls; it also included a 600-seat educational conference center.

Karl Vogt, who served as acting provost and vice president for operations under Olscamp, stated, "Of the three presidents that I've been with, President Olscamp is more open, more honest … I know personally where I stand, whereas [with] previous presidents I wasn't sure at any one point in time where I stood."

During his first two years, Olscamp made significant progress toward reforming the administrative and governance structure and reordering priorities. Presidents traditionally tinker with the organization of the administration, but Olscamp undertook the most substantial reorganization in the University's history, notably by delegating much of the previously centralized authority of provost to vice presidents. The provost office itself was converted into the office of vice president of academic affairs, while budgetary and student affairs responsibilities were elevated from the vice provost level to newly established vice presidencies. Olscamp continued the offices of vice president of operations and vice president of University relations, and their incumbents George Postich and Richard Edwards respectively (although both would be replaced within three years). In the spring of 1983, he named three vice presidents, including two women who became the highest-ranking female officers in the University's history: Eloise E. Clark (academic affairs) and Mary M. Edmonds (student affairs).

When the search for vice president of academic affairs began, Olscamp spoke of his preference for a "female scientist" and Clark, a nationally recognized biologist, brought more impressive credentials to the position than any previous chief academic officer. She had been an officer at the National Science Foundation since 1969, most recently as assistant director for biological, behavioral and social sciences. Edmonds, a physical therapist, had served since 1981 as dean of the College of Health and Community Services. In addition, Eakin moved from student affairs to the vice president for planning and budgeting. The appointments of Clark and Edmonds made an important statement, but many in the student affairs area questioned Edmonds' qualifications and criticized what they saw as the president's office intervening in the search process in her favor. After a difficult start, Edmonds generally worked out well running student affairs; eventually she left Bowling Green to assume a comparable position at Stanford University.

To some observers, this reorganization suggested a reduction of the status of the chief academic officer. Olscamp, however, insisted that this arrangement freed the vice president for academic affairs–whom all vice presidents recognized was the "first among equals"–from reforming the budgetary system and enabled her to concentrate on fulfilling academic initiatives. Budgeting and planning were, in Olscamp's words, "so primitive and yet so complex that it was going to take a great [deal] of work by one person and a staff to develop a system for planning and budgeting that was participatory and that worked here.

"I had clearly in my own mind, the goal of expansion of the graduate school and increasing the commitment to research and graduate work relative to the past, and I thought that was going to occupy the academic vice president," Olscamp said.

Clark took a low-key approach, which annoyed some faculty, but as one board member said, "That was probably what Paul wanted, because he wanted to be his own chief academic officer."

During his first year, Olscamp worked with the Faculty Senate leadership in revising the Academic Charter in ways that enhanced the academic policy and budgetary authority of the senate and increased the role of the faculty in a comprehensive budgeting and planning system. The Academic Council, which had been the principal curricular body, was eliminated with its functions taken over by two newly established groups–the Undergraduate Council and the Senate Committee on Academic Affairs. The budgetary process was built on three-year "rolling" operating budgets and five-year capital budgets; faculty, through representation on newly established collegiate budget committees, a centralized University Budget Committee and a Faculty Senate Budget Committee, were instrumental in determining priorities. On April 19, 1983, the senate overwhelmingly approved the revised charter, with 56 members voting in favor and only one dissenting vote; the required faculty ratification followed, also by a substantial 244-40 margin. These changes remain largely in place.

Olscamp's commitment to enhancing faculty research led to another priority of his first year: reform of salary increment policy. For several years this had been based on the "80-20 formula" (80 percent of the annual salary pool allocated for a percentage across-the-board increase and 20 percent set aside to recognize merit as determined by departments/schools). Olscamp, members of the Board of Trustees and many faculty members believed that the preponderant "across-the-board" component limited recognition of outstanding faculty performance and was actually a disincentive. Olscamp and many other critics of the "80-20 formula" would have preferred a 100 percent merit policy, but that was not politically feasible, so reform came in a proposed "60-40 formula," thus doubling the merit allocation. At the same meeting at which the revised charter was approved, the senate endorsed the "60-40 formula" for a one-year trial, and then in 1984, the senate approved by a 44-15 margin the recommendation that the "60-40 percent formula" be "continued with continuous review."

Presidents traditionally tinker with the organization of the administration, but Olscamp undertook the most substantial reorganization in the University's history ...

With the revised charter and budgeting/planning and salary policies in place, Olscamp set out to remedy the fact that "there wasn't any role and mission statement at all, period." Never before had the University undertaken a comprehensive effort to define its objectives. In the fall of 1983, Olscamp appointed a 15-member Role and Mission Committee, chaired by Arthur Neal of the sociology department who was vice chair of the Faculty Senate, which included faculty, students, administration and trustees representation. It was, however, a predominantly faculty committee–and moreover, a research-oriented faculty–that drafted the statement; the nine faculty members included several high profile researchers, as were several co-chairs of seven subcommittees.

More than 100 faculty members were involved in the process. After several months' work, the committee presented its proposed Role and Mission Statement at the Faculty

Senate meetings on April 24 and May 1, 1984. It encountered considerable criticism for, in the words of one senator, "a lack of balance between the undergraduate and graduate education programs." A dissenting report from the Role and Mission Subcommittee on Undergraduate Education reinforced the criticism, emphasizing a number of unaddressed shortcomings in the undergraduate curriculum. A majority of senators concurred, which resulted in the addition of a new goal that endorsed the University's historic mission: "To maintain and enhance the excellence of undergraduate education, which is and should remain the cornerstone of the institution." The statement also incorporated additional concerns of the undergraduate education subcommittee. The Senate also modified the draft statement's objective of "doubl[ing]" the number of graduate students to "increase[ing] substantially" their numbers. With these modifications addressing the "imbalance" criticism, the senate overwhelmingly endorsed the revised Role and Mission Statement: 61 in favor, one opposed and two abstaining.

As was underscored by the strong senate support for Olscamp's priorities during his first two years, he generally worked effectively with its leaders. Betty van der Smissen (health, physical education and recreation), the senate vice chair, chair of the Charter Revision Committee in 1982-83 and Senate chair in 1983-84, was instrumental in reconciling differences and gaining support for the changes. Olscamp later reflected on her role:

" Betty accomplished a remarkable thing in her term as chair of the Faculty Senate. In spite of suspicion against me, lack of understanding, Betty in one year guided the Faculty Senate through a set of proposals as controversial, as broad, as sweeping, as far ranging, as anything that the Senate has ever considered in its history and they were all voted on. Those include everything from merit salary proposals to these great proposals for change in the relative size of the undergraduate and graduate student body. At the time, everybody cheered politely for her, but in the long run, she, I think, will go down in the history of this University as a pivotal person at a pivotal point in time. "

The senate-approved Role and Mission Statement clearly identified graduate programs and research as the principal areas of future development. In the end, the 27 goals included: "to increase substantially the number of graduate students over the next decade ... to improve and enhance the graduate programs research and graduate programs that already exist ... to initiate new Ph.D. programs in selected areas ... to initiate new programs at the master's level ... to support and enhance the environment in which research takes place ... to mobilize and enhance the research and scholarly activity of the faculty ... to maximize the creative productivity and teaching effectiveness of the faculty, a policy of differential departmental and individual teaching loads should be instituted ... to upgrade and maintain library, equipment, laboratory and other resources necessary for teaching and research ... to significantly increase the level of external funding for research and education. ..." At the undergraduate level, the statement called for making the University the first choice of outstanding students, significantly increasing academic-based scholarships, enhancing the curriculum's "international and intercultural dimension," and fulfilling the decade-old objective of a "practical liberal education."

The graduate/research commitments were reinforced by reallocation of resources and by external recognition. The level of state funding from 1983-88 roughly doubled that of the previous five years, and the added resources were devoted principally to supporting graduate programs, research and the library (the holdings doubled during that period). In addition, in November 1983, Bowling Green was accepted as a member of the National Association of State Universities and Land-Grant Colleges—a designation which was based on the quality of faculty research, strength of doctoral programs and level of external support for research. As Olscamp told the Board of Trustees, "The University has joined the ranks of some of the most prestigious colleges and universities in the country."

That recognition was enhanced by two inter-related developments: the launching of two new Ph.D. programs and the Ohio Board of Regents establishment of the Selective Excellence Program. The new doctorates—in applied philosophy and photochemical sciences—built on existing strengths and concentrated resources on specialized areas within traditional disciplines. The philosophy department had gained national recognition through the Philosophy Documentation Center, the Social Philosophy and Policy Center (established in 1981 with the support of the Stranahan Foundation, and directed by Dr. Fred Miller), and the reorientation of its curriculum to an "applied" approach. These programs had brought $1.5 million in external grants between 1978 and 1984, and the proposal for the doctorate in applied philosophy was developed with the support of a $30,000 grant from the Exxon Education Foundation. In 1985, the Board of Regents approved the Ph.D. program in applied philosophy.

That same year the Center for Photochemical Sciences was established, under the leadership of Douglas C. Neckers who had been chair of the chemistry department since 1974. The center was started to provide training for post-doctoral students and other professionals in the principles of photochemistry, photophysics and spectroscopy as its relates to photochemical processes and polymer chemistry. This was the first photochemical sciences program in the nation to focus on training in an interdisciplinary setting. The visibility of the center was a critical step toward a doctoral program. Within two years, the Board of Trustees endorsed the offering of the Doctor of Philosophy in photochemical sciences—the first such program in the nation—and one that the board found especially attractive because of its importance and relevance to private industry. OBOR gave its approval in 1988.

These new doctoral programs, as well as some of the older ones and to a lesser extent select master's and undergraduate programs, benefited from an important initiative of the Ohio Board of Regents: the Selective Excellence Program. This ambitious undertaking endeavored to direct funds into programs at the state universities, which held the promise of making Ohio pre-eminent in some of the "most vital fields of higher education." Behind the program was pressure from the Ohio General Assembly for OBOR to strengthen good programs and inactivate or restructure the less productive ones. Beginning in 1979, the General Assembly requested that OBOR make "recommendations for developing excellence in specific programs … and relate such recommendations to specific institutions of higher education." Leaders in the General Assembly and Governor Richard Celeste, who was elected in 1982, supported incentives for quality

enhancement. The Selective Excellence Program envisioned public universities building "centers of excellence" to serve as magnets for attracting top-flight scholars and students. OBOR endorsed an enrichment program "to allow this state to invest in its winners."

Toward that end, OBOR established: 1) the Eminent Scholars program, based on a statewide competition and first funded in the 1983-85 biennium; it provided endowed professorship on a matching basis into already strong academic departments "which could be propelled into the first-rank through the addition of a scholar-leader of national or international visibility"; 2) Program Excellence, also launched in 1983-85, which provided for enhancement of select undergraduate programs, challenging colleges and universities to put forward for state competition their strongest undergraduate programs; 3) the Research Challenge program, designed to replace outdated equipment; 4) the Academic Challenge program, which began in the 1985-87 biennium and provided each state university with grants equivalent to 1 percent of the institution's subsidy to be used for ongoing funding of "selective advancement of academic programs" based on internal competition and selection, subject to final OBOR approval.

BGSU's photochemical sciences program was the first in the nation to focus on training in an interdisciplinary setting.

Hockey's Greatest Moment: The NCAA Championship

On March 24, 1984, the hockey team won the NCAA hockey championship in a thrilling, four-overtime 5-4 victory over the University of Minnesota-Duluth (UMD).

The victory came 20 years after the hockey program started as a club sport at BGSU. After the Ice Arena opened in 1969, hockey became an intercollegiate sport for the Falcons. BGSU soon became a major power and in 1983-84 won its third straight Central Collegiate Hockey Association (CCHA) championship. Winning 17 straight games at one point and ranked number 1 in the country for six weeks, BGSU slumped in the CCHA play-offs and received an at-large invitation to the eight-team NCAA field. After defeating Boston University, BGSU squared off with CCHA-rival Michigan State in the semi-finals and defeated the Spartans, 2-1, before advancing to the finals against UMD.

That set the stage for perhaps the most exciting collegiate hockey game in history. UMD led 4-2 with eight minutes remaining. A goal by Peter Wilson pulled the Falcons to within one goal, and with less than two minutes remaining, John Samanski scored the tying goal. Then began three agonizing 10-minute overtimes, during which the BGSU goalie Gary Kruzich made 13 saves and his UMD counterpart made 14. Then seven minutes into the fourth overtime, Gino Cavallini's backhand shot slipped the puck between the goalie and post and found the nets for the victory.

The BGSU Falcon hockey team brought home the national championship trophy in 1984.

The Academic Challenge program benefited select doctoral and some master's programs. Of the approximate $3.3 million awarded the University over three biennia (all Selective Excellence programs ended with the 1989-91 biennium), about 85 percent was allocated for enhancing graduate programs. In the first round grants, announced in early 1986, the University supported the emerging doctoral programs in chemistry for its photochemical sciences program and philosophy for its applied philosophy program, as well as established programs in the sociology department for its applied demography program and the psychology department for clinical psychology. The other awards were made to the master's programs in college student personnel and management. The two additional rounds of funding announced in 1988 and 1990 provided second grants to the Ph.D. programs in photochemistry, philosophy/social philosophy, the policy center and psychology for organizational psychology, as well as to the doctoral programs in biological sciences for its focus on genetics and molecular biology, history for its concentration on policy history, and mathematics and statistics. Also receiving Academic Challenge support were the undergraduate and master's level programs in the College of Musical Arts, the computer science and marketing departments, and the two-year programs at Firelands. The annual grants were added to the ongoing budgets of the departments and helped the long-term building of these areas.

The University fared reasonably well in the statewide undergraduate-centered Program Excellence competition. Beneficiaries included the departments of chemistry, psychology, management, visual communication technology and computer science.

The new doctoral programs and the long-esteemed psychology program each gained Eminent Scholars. The statewide competition, which funded approximately one in 10 proposals, provided a $500,000 endowment grant that had to be matched by a $500,000 commitment from the host university. Among 36 appointments approved during the four biennia of the program—mostly to more comprehensive universities and the hard sciences—17 went to Ohio State University and 10 to the University of Cincinnati; eight of all the appointments were in the humanities and social sciences. In 1987 Michael Rodgers, a specialist in laser photochemistry and the director of the Center for Fast Kinetics Research at the University of Texas in Austin, became Bowling Green's first Eminent Scholar. Within the next four years, he was joined by two others: Edward McClennen, who came from Washington University in St. Louis, as an Eminent Scholar in philosophy specializing in decision and game theory, and Milton D. Hakel, who came from the University of Houston, as an Eminent Scholar in industrial and organizational psychology. With three Eminent Scholars, Bowling Green matched Ohio University in the number of awards to the "second tier" state universities (two were awarded to the University of Akron and one to Miami University).

By the end of Olscamp's presidency, 25 members of the faculty had been honored for their scholarship or creative work ...

The doctorates in applied philosophy and photochemical sciences were "new" programs, although technically the number of Ph.D. programs increased by five—from nine to 14—during the Olscamp presidency. The other additions reflected the "unbundling" of four graduate programs that had been housed in the School of Speech Communication, which had all offered doctorates under the "speech communication" designation. With the dissolution of the School of Speech Communication, each of its constituent parts—interpersonal and public communications, theatre, mass communication and communications disorders—became distinct entities.

Olscamp's commitment to the research mission was reflected in enhanced recognition of faculty accomplishments. In 1985, he and his wife established the Paul and Ruth Olscamp Research Award, which is presented annually to a faculty member for outstanding research or creative accomplishments over a three-year period—the first such university-wide recognition. In 1989, Olscamp hosted the first faculty recognition dinner, which became an annual event in the fall, to recognize faculty for their years of service and to present major faculty awards—the Olscamp Research Award, Master Teaching Award and Distinguished Faculty Service Award.

Olscamp also was instrumental in establishing the title of Distinguished Research/Artist Professor, which is "conferred upon select members of the faculty … who have established outstanding national or international recognition throughout research and publications or creative/artistic achievement in their disciplines." The criteria for this appointment are similar to those of the previously established Distinguished University Professorships, but this title clarifies the emphasis on research/artistic accomplishment.

Given his commitment to scholarship, it was fitting that Olscamp presided over the most extensive faculty recognition in the University's history. In 1986 Douglas Neckers was named the first Distinguished Research Professor. During Olscamp's presidency, six other faculty were so honored: Jaak Panksepp, psychology (1989); Gary R. Hess, history (1990); Philip F. O' Connor, English (1991); Charles Holland, mathematics and statistics (1993), and Ronny C. Woodruff, biological sciences (1994). Olscamp continued to recognize Distinguished University Professors by holding University-wide convocations for the conferral of these titles.

Olscamp also presided over the designation of nine new Distinguished University Professors: Robert Guion, psychology (1982); Orlando C. Behling, management (1986); Pietro Badia, psychology (1986); Arthur G. Neal, sociology (1987); Lawrence J. Friedman, history (1991); Michael Doherty, psychology (1992); Chan Hahn, management (1994); Kenneth Kiple, history (1994); and Arjun J. Gupta, mathematics and statistics (1995).

By the end of Olscamp's presidency, 25 members of the faculty had been honored for their scholarship or creative work, including the three Eminent Scholars and Ohio Regents Scholar John Paul Scott. Eighteen of those titles were conferred during the Olscamp presidency.

Near the end of his presidency, as external support for research in the arts and humanities declined, Olscamp promised support from the University's internal endowment to establish the Institute for the Study of Culture, Society and Human Values (later modified to the Institute for the Study of Culture and Society). Since its launching in 1995-96, the institute has provided up to six one-semester leaves per academic year to enable selected tenured faculty to concentrate on scholarly and creative projects.

Although Olscamp never pushed for undergraduate curricular reform despite his strong convictions about the importance of traditional liberal arts in general education, he attempted to enhance the undergraduate program by recruiting national merit scholars. A program of scholarships for such students enabled Bowling Green to rank by the late 1980s among the top 50 schools in the country (and in 1989 the best in Ohio) in enrolling freshmen national merit scholars.

The significance of undergraduate education was also reflected in efforts to recognize outstanding teachers. The Master Teacher Award was established in 1982 and has been awarded annually ever since; it is based on student nominations with the decision made by a student award committee. In addition, the designation of research professorships provided impetus for teaching professorships. Originating with several faculty members and deans, the proposal to establish Distinguished Teaching Professors to recognize faculty with outstanding achievements in the classroom won the support of Olscamp and the Faculty Senate. Distinguished Teaching Professorships were established in 1989 with M. Neil Browne of the economics department the first faculty member so honored. During Olscamp's presidency, four others received the title: Chan Hahn, management (1990); Virginia Marks, music performance studies (1991); V. Frederick Rickey, mathematics and statistics, (1992); Lee Meserve, biological sciences (1993).

In 1985 the College of Technology was established, marking a milestone in undergraduate curriculum. Under the leadership of Jerry Streichler, the School of Technology had outgrown the constraints of being housed in the College of Education. College status enabled degrees to be offered in technology and architecture and developed a curriculum that stresses "hands-on" experiences with required semester-long cooperative programs.

From the beginning, Olscamp pressed to develop a program in Canadian Studies; by 1991, BGSU had established the Canadian Studies Center. This interest reflected Olscamp's Canadian heritage, yet more broadly he believed that Bowling Green, given its proximity to the Great Lakes and Canada, could foster Americans' awareness of Canada's importance and economic and cultural collaboration between the state of Ohio and Canada. In 1982 a course on Canadian history constituted the extent of the "Canadian curriculum," but several courses on Canadian affairs were established in the next few years, enabling students to minor in the field. Facilitating this development were several grants from the Canadian government and annual appropriations, beginning in 1989, from the State of Ohio. With extensive holdings of Canadian documents and secondary works, coupled with faculty and student research and various programs, most notably the annual Reddin Symposium, the center became prominent in promoting Canadian-American collaboration.

Meanwhile, faculty discontent at Firelands forced an effort to improve the relationship between the main campus and Firelands. During the early years of the Firelands Campus, academic departments looked upon it as an extension of the main campus, seeking to integrate, if not control, course offerings and assuming a primary role in recruitment and evaluation of faculty. Faculty at Firelands resented being treated, as one put it, as a "farm club" of the main campus. When Firelands was elevated to college status in 1976, the college had its own dean and departments, providing greater autonomy and an enhanced status. In essence, the change acknowledged that responsibilities and expectations of faculty in a two-year college differed significantly from those in a four-year university. At the same time, however, collegiate status did not bring, in the opinion

The College of Technology was welcomed in 1985, offering a curriculum that stressed "hands-on" experiences.

of Firelands faculty and staff, recognition as peers of the main campus faculty. In December 1985, the Firelands faculty endorsed a statement on the college's goals, which affirmed that it was "much more than a community college … [and] seeks to be the premier institution fostering liberal arts education in north central Ohio." It was also committed and mandated by OBOR and the state legislature, to provide technological education to meet the needs of the local community—which, many at Firelands saw as leading to the impression that it was little more than a community college. In an effort to address the Firelands faculty, staff and students "wish to correct misperceptions and to be no longer viewed as a liability, but rather … be welcomed as colleagues and fellow students," a committee recommended in 1987 a number of measures designed to enhance communication, to integrate certain programs and administrative functions, and to enhance understanding on the main campus of the Firelands mission and programs.

Beyond the world of academic programs and problems, it was a great time for Falcon athletics. The hockey team provided Bowling Green with its ultimate achievement of an NCAA championship. Between 1982 and 1992, the football team made four bowl appearances. Under Coach Denny Stolz, the Falcons regained prominence in the MAC, winning titles in 1982 and 1985, with the latter team going undefeated (11-0) through the regular season, which earned visits to the California Bowl. The results were disappointing. In 1982, Fresno State rallied to win on a last-minute touchdown and even more devastating was the 1985 re-match with Fresno State, which manhandled the previously unbeaten Falcons, 51-7. Stolz announced a few days before the game that he was leaving Bowling Green for another coaching position; it became a major distraction.

By the early 1990s, coach Gary Blackney rebuilt the Falcons into MAC champions in 1991 and 1992 and led them to victories in the California Raisin Bowl, finally defeating Fresno State, and in the Las Vegas Bowl, defeating Nevada.

Also during Olscamp's presidency, the development of support for women's teams, thanks in large part to Title IX, changed the character of intercollegiate athletics.

President Olscamp's interest in Canada resulted in the start of Canadian studies program led by Dr. Mark Kasoff and the Reddin Symposium.

Transformative leaders often face opposition. From the beginning of his administration, Olscamp encountered an undercurrent of criticism. Reflecting both divisive substantive issues and reactions to his leadership style, the opposition became more widespread and outspoken, culminating in a "no-confidence" movement in 1990.

This meant that 30 years after the McDonald controversy, another Bowling Green president faced a serious faculty challenge. The Faculty Senate introduced a "no-confidence" resolution on Jan. 16, 1990, forcing a contentious showdown within the senate and across campus. Similar to 1961, aggrieved faculty in 1990 contended that the president was acting arbitrarily in ways that harmed the University and ignored the prerogatives of the faculty. In both cases, there was an underlying resistance to the changes brought by a president who pressed the University in the direction of greater commitment to research and graduate education. In 1986 interviews, two faculty members expressed concerns over the University's direction and leadership. One spoke wistfully of the loss of the undergraduate teaching mission:

" *We are never going to be able to go back to the style of leadership that Hollis Moore had. There seemed to be on the part of the faculty much higher morale and less criticism of the administration. Today there seems to be a lot more dissension among the ranks … maybe even lower morale … We've changed from an institution that was primarily teacher-oriented, teacher education-oriented basically.* "

Another longtime professor drew a direct comparison to McDonald:

" *I think that in many respects Olscamp is going back to the dictatorial approach that McDonald had. … It seems that Olscamp is having those things changed back to where he really ends up with the final say more so than the committee approach, which was more the main avenue or thrust or direction [under Jerome and Moore].* "

There was one link between the "rebels" of 1961 and 1990: Virginia B. Platt, professor emeritus of history, was appointed to the Board of Trustees in 1984 and became a frequent critic of Olscamp's leadership. Thirty years earlier, she and her late husband, Grover C. Platt, had been prominent in the anti-McDonald movement. As a member of the board, she defined her mission as one of upholding the system of faculty governance that had been put in place after McDonald's resignation and which she believed Olscamp was subverting.

Criticism of Olscamp's leadership gained momentum during the late 1980s, as his critics gained influence in the Faculty Senate. Despite his accomplishments and his claims to commitment to shared governance, Olscamp was consistently regarded by a number of faculty as acting arbitrarily. In his first year in office, he had implemented without faculty input a "solicitation" policy that restricted the use of campus mail and other means of communication for non-university business (which critics saw as restricting the American Association of University Professors or other groups from engaging in any faculty union activities). Differences over the "solicitation" issue were seemingly resolved, but the incident lingered as an example, to his critics, of presidential abuse of power. In November 1986 the Board of Trustees approved the "gag rule," which stipulated that the president had to be invited to any meeting of faculty with three of more of its members. Critics viewed the rule as a reflection of Olscamp's annoyance with faculty who had met privately with board members to question the costs of a new telecommunications system. The following year the senate established an Oppression Committee to investigate charges of intimidation by the administration against its critics, which Olscamp privately dismissed as "a lot of nonsense." These matters and other allegations against the administration became a matter of public attention when a series of articles critical of the Olscamp administration appeared in the *Lorain Journal* in the fall of 1987. In the aftermath of this unfavorable publicity, a group of faculty—the Committee of Concerned Faculty—addressed an open letter to the University community in January 1988. Defending the proposition that "teaching and research are essential and inseparable components of academic excellence," the letter criticized the "negative, divisive and adversarial" actions of the Senate Executive Committee that "interfere with [the] pursuit of excellence. … The charge that 'an oppressive atmosphere' exists … is totally groundless and embarrassingly ludicrous."

Undeterred by calls for restraint, the Faculty Senate leadership pressed its case. Bartley Brennan of the legal studies department and Ann Marie Lancaster of the computer science department, who were senate chairs in 1988-89 and 1989-90, respectively, had particularly contentious relationships with Olscamp, which set the stage for the "no-confidence" resolution. The senate leadership in 1988-89 questioned the administration's commitment to assuring the safe working conditions of custodial staff. They called upon Olscamp to survey faculty and staff on the adequacy of emergency room care at Wood County Hospital, and challenged his plan to establish a single personnel office and to place it under the vice president of operations, Karl Vogt, who was also a frequent target of senate leadership criticism.

… 30 years after the McDonald controversy, another Bowling Green president faced a serious faculty challenge.

When Olscamp, without consulting the senate, appointed a faculty member to serve on a committee to study the feasibility of the proposed personnel office, the senate officers wrote a memo accusing him of an "arbitrary and capricious" action. Olscamp responded that such charges, if made publicly, would be libelous and he would act accordingly; in response, Brennan said he hoped that Olscamp's message was not intended to "create a chilling effect." In addition, the senate officers tried to force the Board of Trustees to receive certain senate resolutions as "action" rather than "information" items, which Melvin Murray, as chair of the board, rejected on the grounds that the board was concerned with "policy-making and [was] not interested in the intricacies or mechanics of policies." To many members of the board, the senate leadership seemed arrogant and over-reaching, which tended to make them more defensive of Olscamp. By the fall of 1989 when Lancaster became chair, the senate leadership was challenging Olscamp's "unilateral" imposition of a campus-wide no-smoking policy as a violation of the Faculty Charter and Senate resolutions.

The long-simmering differences worsened in December 1989 when Lancaster exchanged sharp words with Olscamp—which became widely known—over his appointment of Phillip R. Mason as vice president for University relations. Mason had been serving since 1982 as executive assistant to the president and secretary of the Board of Trustees, having followed Olscamp to Bowling Green from Western Washington University. Lancaster charged that Olscamp had ignored affirmative action procedures and warned that she would do anything in her power to stop the appointment, which she characterized as "simply a perpetuation of the 'old boys network' approach to vice-presidential appointments." In response, Olscamp defended the practice of presidential appointments, without benefit of national searches, in the case of non-academic vice presidents, pointing as precedent to his appointments of Vogt and Eakin as vice presidents of planning and budgeting and operations, respectively, and to his predecessor's appointment of Edwards as vice president of University relations. Olscamp, however, had conducted national searches in other cases, notably in the appointments of Dwight Burlingame to replace Edwards in 1985, and Robert Martin as Vogt's successor in 1988; moreover his hiring of Mason in 1982, to fill essentially a staff position, had also been conducted through a national search. This inconsistent record supported Olscamp's point that the nature of such appointments was a presidential prerogative. In this case, however, Olscamp invited criticism because it did appear to be the "old-boys' network" and Mason's qualifications for the position were questionable. One member of the board later commented that it was a "bad choice."

The controversy over Mason's appointment was the catalyst for the no-confidence resolution. Prior to the senate meeting of Jan. 16, 1990, members had no advance knowledge of the resolution, which was not included in the agenda; neither did Olscamp, who was out of town, and, in his own word, was "blind-sided." At the meeting, Lancaster, after a series of customary reports, announced that the senate officers (the others being vice Chair Blaine Ritts (accounting and management information systems) and secretary Benjamin N. Muego (Firelands) had changed the remainder of the agenda. She introduced the issue of the Mason appointment, reporting that 70 percent of the faculty who responded to a questionnaire on the matter believed "that the Faculty Senate should continue voicing objections to [the] action." Utilizing a series of graphs, she portrayed the administration's "disregard" for undergraduate instruction through its increasing reliance on temporary faculty and graduate students for instruction in lower-division undergraduate classes; in the fall of 1989, only 38 percent of such sections were taught by probationary or tenured faculty.

Lancaster read a strongly worded and caustic indictment of Olscamp's leadership, which essentially charged that favored programs were being supported while undergraduate education was being short-changed. The staffing picture demonstrated ill-considered priorities:

" *If the University allocates only a meager amount to the teaching of freshman courses, what is it saying? It is saying, this particular endeavor is not a high priority—it is not very important. [Olscamp and Clark] will not recognize that there is a problem. Why? Do they really believe that we all are collectively hallucinating? ... The Role and Mission Statement ... is not a planning document. It is our collective sketch of an ideal academic institution where we can "do it all" ... [Olscamp refuses] to come to terms with the fact that we cannot do everything and so we have not specified which goals are beyond our reach. ... The President has built a façade—a hollow structure. Monies have been allocated to 'high profile' items with emphasis on the glitz. Moneys have consistently been allocated to items mandated by the President without instituting monitoring and valuation mechanisms.* "

At what point, she asked rhetorically, would the staffing picture and the priorities reflected therein, reach an "unacceptable" level? The crisis was at hand: "We have allowed ourselves to become desensitized to the outrageous." The Academic Charter gives "the faculty ... the primary authority and responsibility to develop, sustain and enhance the intellectual quality and reputation of the institution and maintain its academic integrity." Lancaster concluded: "I am suggesting that while it may be a bit late, we begin assuming that responsibility."

When Lancaster finished, Ritts introduced the "no-confidence" resolution. Premised on the claim that the senate officers spent "the majority of their time responding to unilateral actions of the president" and that their responsibility was " to insure that faculty interests are properly considered and protected because normal channels for shared governance are disregarded and/or violated," the resolution called for the senate to express "no confidence in the continued leadership and management of University affairs by Paul J. Olscamp." If approved by the senate, the resolution would then be submitted to all faculty. If a majority supported the resolution by Jan. 25, it would be forwarded to the Board of Trustees. An attached "bill of particulars" listed 10 charges against Olscamp, which were placed in three categories: violations of academic freedom and free expression, violations of shared governance processes, and lack of competence in financial and administrative affairs.

It was the most dramatic moment in the senate's history. Its officers were calling upon senators to demand the president's resignation. The majority of senators refused to be rushed into supporting a measure of such magnitude. Lancaster's statement regarding the staffing/ budgetary situation and each of the 10 "particulars" warranted serious consideration and debate. There seemed to be a "disconnect" between Lancaster's criticisms and the call for no confidence. Were Olscamp's "misdeeds" of such magnitude as to justify "no confidence" in his presidency? Moreover, fairness dictated that Olscamp deserved an opportunity to respond. As a result, the officers failed to gain the anticipated senate backing. The body voted (25-21) to table the resolution.

Underlying the senate's reaction was its leadership's lack of political acumen. It was unrealistic to expect a majority of the senate to approve a no-confidence resolution with virtually no time for debate. Equally ill considered was the follow-up procedure of a faculty referendum within 10 days, which ignored such fundamental points as procedure and eligibility, and failed to provide opportunity for debate.

The no-confidence resolution triggered criticism of the senate officers. Telling his staff "this is war," Olscamp returned to town and prepared to take the offensive, but for the first few

The 75th Anniversary Celebration: 'An Environment For Excellence'

The University celebrated its 75th anniversary during the 1985-86 academic year. Kicked off by the President's opening day address on Aug. 26, 1985 and concluding with commencement in May 1986, the anniversary's theme "An Environment for Excellence" was commemorated during the year at a number of traditional activities, including Homecoming, Parent's Day and Alumni-Faculty Day. The "Environment for Excellence" theme was considered an appropriate sequence to the 50th anniversary theme: "Education Our Challenge, Excellence Our Goal."

The celebration reflected the work of a 26-member committee headed by Larry Weiss, assistant vice president for university relations and director of alumni affairs, which was to "commemorate and celebrate [without going] overboard." That reflected the sentiment of Olscamp and most of the committee, that a 75th celebration ought not be comparable in scale to a 50th or 100th anniversary. The 75th anniversary committee had one notable link to the 1960 celebration for it included John Davidson, emeritus professor of marketing, who had served as executive secretary of the 50th Anniversary Celebration Committee.

The major event was a convocation held on Sunday, Nov. 10, 1985, which marked the 75th anniversary of Bowling Green's selection as the site of the new school in northwest Ohio. Held in Memorial Hall and with Olscamp presiding, the convocation included speeches by Bowling Green mayor (and emeritus faculty member) Bruce Bellard, Ohio Board of Regents Chancellor William Coulter and former president Jerome, with the keynote address by 1959 graduate Charles Perry, president

of Golden Bear International, the Florida-based marketing organization of golfer Jack Nicklaus.

In addition, the anniversary was marked by the publication of *The Falcon Soars*, a history of the University since 1963 written by Stuart Givens of the history department, an oral history project which involved interviews of prominent figures in the University's history and preserved in the University's archives, and a photographic exhibit in McFall Center depicting the changes in campus over the years.

What distinguished the 75th anniversary from earlier ones was a major fundraising effort: a $12.5 million 75th anniversary fund was announced at the convocation. By the time that the campaign ended on June 30, 1987, more than $15.2 million had been raised. Included were gifts, each of $1 million, from Harold and Helen McMaster of Perrysburg to establish the McMaster Institute and the Stranahan Foundation of Toledo to support the Social Philosophy and Policy Center; other major gifts included the endowing of the Ashel G. Bryan/ Mid-American Bank Professorship in Finance in recognition of Bryan's service to the University; the funding of a $3.65 million addition to the Business Administration Building from the Owens-Corning Fiberglass Corporation, Dana Corporation and 1951 alumnus James R. Good; an endowed scholarship by actress and alumna Eva Marie Saint; support from actress Lillian Gish to support the Dorothy and Lillian Gish Film Theater; gifts from the Mead Corporation and the Paul and Diana Block Foundation to support the Center for Photochemical Sciences.

Harold and Helen McMaster have been generous donors to BGSU, starting in 1985 with the 75th anniversary fund and continuing into the 21st century.

The Emergence of Women's Basketball

Women at BGSU began playing basketball on an intercollegiate basis during the 1962-63 season under Coach Dorothy Luedtke. However the roots of women's basketball at BG go back much further, to the very beginning of the institution's history.

1914 > During the first year of classes, two literary societies, the Wilsonian and the Emerson, which were both cultural and social societies, established women's basketball teams that played each other.

1924 > There were interclass basketball tournaments for women and competition for spots on the roster was keen. The freshman team had more than 50 candidates try out for the team.

1935-36 > Standout athlete Margaret Hurlburt captained the campus championship teams in women's basketball, field hockey and soccer.

1938 > The Women's Physical Education Building opened. The previous campus gymnasium was located in the Administration Building (today known as University Hall) in what is today the Joe E. Brown Theater.

1943 > Faculty member Gertrude Eppler formed women's sports clubs.

1947-48 > Women were divided into 20 campus basketball teams with 10 teams in each league.

1962-63 > Although BGSU had an extensive program of intramural sports for every undergraduate women student, the basketball program, under Coach Dorothy Luedtke, began playing on an intercollegiate basis.

1972 > Title IX became Federal law and its passage created many new opportunities for female athletes.

1973-74 > One of the most successful early teams at BG was Coach Sue Hager's '73-'74 team which went 12-4 including convincing wins of 63-34 over Miami, 77-30 over Kent and 62-39 over Toledo.

1981-82 > This BG team, under Coach Kathy Bole, was the first Falcon women's basketball squad to compete in Mid-American Conference play.

1986-87 > Under Coach Fran Voll, BGSU went through the MAC regular season and tournament play unbeaten to capture the first conference titles in school history.

1988-89 > On March 15, 1989, Anderson Arena hosted an NCAA Tournament game for the first time. A sellout crowd of over 4,100 cheered the Falcons to a 69-59 victory over Cincinnati.

2001 > Curt Miller becomes the ninth head coach in women's history and ushers in a new era of tremendous success.

> *Larry Weiss '67*

The BGSU women's basketball team hosted an NCAA Tournament game for the first time in 1989 and celebrated a 69-59 victory over Cincinnati.

days, he wisely allowed others to speak out against the senate leadership. The day after the senate meeting, Warren Hall, president of the Board of Trustees, issued a strong statement: "Speaking on behalf of the board, I am surprised by this motion and particularly dismayed that it was presented in Dr. Olscamp's absence. I cannot say strongly enough that the board believes that we have an outstanding president." The board, by an 8-1 vote (Virginia Platt being the only dissenter), expressed its lack of confidence in the senate officers.

The president of the Undergraduate Student Government, Kevin Coughlin, called for that body to support Olscamp and to condemn the Faculty Senate's leadership whose actions "were a thinly veiled attack by people who have had it in for him for a while." An open letter by four former Faculty Senate chairs called for the resignations of the senate officers who "have badly misrepresented the attitudes of the faculty at large and have lost the confidence of the administration and Board of Trustees … [O]ur cherished system of shared governance has been placed in grave danger by the actions of the senate officers."

The *BG News* criticized the senate leadership's clumsy approach and lack of diplomacy. A statement by the Bowling Green City leaders praised Olscamp's work in promoting university-community relations. Having over-reached politically and facing much criticism, Lancaster and Ritts resigned their offices on Jan. 23. They agreed to do so in a meeting with Olscamp, during which he rejected Lancaster's overture that she still be "part of the solution to the university's problem" with the rejoinder that the officers' "declaration of war tantamount to a public call for [his] resignation" had closed that door with him and the Board of Trustees.

The next day, Olscamp sent faculty a five-page response to each of the "particulars" supplemented by six appendices; he affirmed that he was "absolutely and irrevocably committed to shared governance." At the Faculty Senate meeting Feb. 6, the administration responded forcefully to the no-confidence resolution. Olscamp described the charges as "mendacious and malevolent … with no foundation whatsoever in fact." He claimed that he had "done more than any president … to enhance and broaden faculty authority and participation in governance," and emphatically denied "accusations and charges that [he had]

intimidated or coerced people, repressed open discussion or free speech or mismanaged in any way the finances of the University." Hall reaffirmed the board's concern; referring to his seven years' experience as chair of the board's finance committee, Hall told the senate that the University was in excellent financial condition, but the unsubstantiated charges in the bill of particulars were "potentially damaging to the University's enrollment and endowment."

… *"I abstain on this vote for the reason that I believe a great deal more can be done to create at this institution an atmosphere of open discussion [and] open relationships …"*

Also presented to the senate were the minutes of the Feb. 2 meeting of the Board of Trustees, which passed a resolution stating both its "deep concern over the current negative atmosphere created by the initiation of the resolution of no confidence … [and its] strong support [of] President Paul J. Olscamp." Then Peter Hutchinson, associate vice president for academic affairs, responded to the claims of disregard for undergraduate education with data purporting to show that Bowling Green had the second-lowest percentage of part-time faculty among Ohio's state-supported universities and that the percentage of teaching done by part-time faculty had been constant over the previous five years.

While the eight other members of the Board of Trustees voted for the Feb. 2 resolution supporting Olscamp, Virginia Platt abstained, stating: "I abstain on this vote for the reason that I believe a great deal more can be done to create at this institution an atmosphere of open discussion, open relationships, and consequently, I want to have on the record that I think we can make a great improvement in that area."

Although the no-confidence resolution remained tabled, the dissidents still led by Lancaster and Ritts, who remained senate members, pressed for consideration of the issues raised in the Bill of Particulars. At the Feb. 6 meeting, the senate approved a resolution for consideration as a "committee of the whole," which was subsequently set for March 27. Prior to that meeting, Lancaster and Ritts distributed materials documenting the "particulars" against Olscamp.

Not to be lost in the furor of early 1990, many faculty shared much of the senate leadership's concerns about academic priorities and the state of undergraduate education. Had the senate leadership acted more astutely by focusing on major budgetary and staffing issues and not pressed for no-confidence based in large part on issues (the 10 "particulars") about which many faculty had little knowledge, it might have forced a debate on significant issues of concern to all faculty.

... Olscamp announced plans for three faculty forums to "discuss ways in which we might improve our general community and scholarly life on the campus."

After its unrecorded "committee of the whole" discussion on March 27 and with "no confidence" no longer a viable course, the Faculty Senate undertook a more widely accepted, if unprecedented, means to assert faculty prerogatives: a systematic faculty evaluation of the president. This process had been discussed earlier, briefly during the Moore presidency and again in 1987 when the senate questioned whether Olscamp's contract calling for the Board of Trustees "to develop written procedures for conducting the periodic review of the president" included a faculty evaluation. A statement in February 1988 from the board chairman William F. Spengler said that the trustees would solicit "input from individuals" on the president's performance, but "the blare of publicity ... associated with formal evaluations ... which may, or may not, represent the consensus of those who represent the constituency" would compromise the board's sole responsibility to evaluate the president. Undeterred, the Faculty Senate voted 57 to 7 on April 3 to conduct an evaluation of Olscamp during the 1990 fall semester. The senate elected a seven-person committee to conduct the only faculty evaluation of the president in the University's first century.

Reaffirming its 1988 statement on its prerogatives, the board on May 11 declined (with Virginia Platt the only dissenting vote) to acknowledge the Faculty Senate resolution to evaluate the president, which foreshadowed its refusal to formally receive the results of the evaluation.

The politics of the "no-confidence" movement remained part of the political culture during the evaluation in the fall of 1990. Lancaster and Ritts sent copies of their document on the "particulars" against Olscamp to all faculty, saying in a cover memorandum that it might be useful in responding to an evaluation questionnaire. In his opening day address in August, Olscamp announced plans for three faculty forums to "discuss ways in which we might improve our general community and scholarly life on the campus." These forums were to be based in part on the recently released "UCLA Study"—a survey of faculty "job satisfaction" at 500 postsecondary institutions, including Bowling Green, which was conduced by the Higher Education Research Institute based at the University of California at Los Angeles. (The survey had been completed prior to the "no-confidence" resolution, with 62 percent of full-time faculty participating.) As Olscamp wrote to the faculty announcing the first of the forums, the UCLA Study showed a "generally quite favorable picture of the working climate here," but also included "some responses which should be of concern to us all."

During the 1990 fall semester, the Presidential Evaluation Committee distributed a form to 698 tenured and probationary faculty, which called for evaluating Olscamp (on a 1-5 scale) in seven categories followed by a single overall assessment of his performance.[1] The results, which were released in December, showed that among the nearly 50 percent of faculty who participated, Olscamp's performance was generally regarded as ranging between "below-average" (2) to "average" (3). His greatest strength was seen as "public relations" (with a 3.17 rating), while the lowest rating was in "decision-making" (2.19). The overall assessment, 2.53, naturally attracted the greatest attention. Among faculty who responded in writing to the question of how Olscamp could increase his effectiveness, most frequently suggested was that

---

1. The author was chair of the Presidential Evaluation Committee.

he change his leadership style through improved communications with faculty and avoidance of confrontational and adversarial tactics. The largely negative results of the evaluation surprised many faculty, who thought, on the basis of the rejection of the no-confidence resolution, that Olscamp enjoyed greater support. That seeming discrepancy can be explained by the fact that much of the adverse reaction to the resolution resulted from its perceived unfairness, not from support of Olscamp.

The results of the evaluation annoyed Olscamp, but he responded to it in an accommodating letter to the faculty. Characterizing the overall rating as "not that good, but … similar to national data," he said "much more disturbing" were low scores and comments regarding "personal and leadership style, rather than policy or operational matters" because "perceptions expressed in the data do not fit at all with my attitude toward you. I am apparently perceived as overly defensive, abrupt, brusque, too aggressive and argumentative and as a bad listener." He went on to mention that he had just signed a contract to serve three more years and that he planned to retire on June 30, 1994. After listing priorities for the remainder of his term, he promised to "improve my personal and leadership style."

The Olscamp letter was notable for what it did not say: he avoided challenging the evaluation process, including the fact that only half of eligible faculty had responded and the lack of any internal or external comparison base; he avoided claiming that many faculty who did not vote opposed the senate playing a role in the president's evaluation; he avoided charging that a false sense of crisis over the Mason appointment had been perpetuated by Olscamp's enemies and influenced the atmosphere in which the evaluation was conducted; he avoided saying that as an "agent of change" he had alienated faculty by bringing new standards and higher performance expectations. These criticisms were all suggested to him as a way of challenging the integrity of the evaluation, but in a wise move politically, Olscamp accepted the results. Yet no matter how graciously he responded, the "below average" rating undermined his effectiveness.

Barely had the publicity of the presidential evaluation ended before a renewed campaign for faculty unionization presented another challenge to the Olscamp administration. A collective bargaining effort had been long anticipated, but the catalyst for action was a 1992 administration plan to reduce summer teaching compensation, which the Faculty Senate denounced in a strongly worded resolution. A poll of faculty in the spring of 1992 showed that among those responding (which constituted more than half of the faculty), over 70 percent favored collective bargaining. Over the next few weeks the Bowling Green Faculty Association (BGFA) gained support as the collective bargaining agent, and its leaders began the process of soliciting the required faculty signatures for the certification of a collective bargaining election. Meanwhile, an opposition group, the Advocates for Academic Independence (AAI), emerged and challenged the need for a faculty union amidst charges from the BGFA that it was a "stooge" for the administration. Procedural questions, including clarification of which faculty were eligible to vote, delayed the process, until finally the election was scheduled for February 1994.

Although the Board of Trustees continually gave him its support publicly, some members … were maneuvering to isolate him from some of its deliberations and to begin looking for his successor.

In the weeks before the election, the debate became increasingly strident: Olscamp, unlike Moore in 1979, took a prominent role, warning that collective bargaining would be "a net loss for faculty" and would "discourage attempts to be outstanding." Ron Stoner (physics), the president of BGFA, responded that faculty "would strive for excellence whether there's collective bargaining or not." He and other leaders, like Ryan Tweney (psychology) and Harold Lunde (management) argued that it was time for the faculty to take control from a "management culture, which ultimately looks at cost cutting in the labor areas." BGFA contended that 60 percent of four-year institutions of higher learning had collective bargaining which faculty found beneficial, and there was no known instance of faculty de-certifying their bargaining agent. On the other side, AAI leaders Milt Hakel (psychology), Stuart Givens (history) and George Clemens (chemistry), among others, questioned—on the basis of the experiences of state universities in Ohio, which had union contracts—whether collective bargaining would yield improvement in faculty salaries. They also foresaw unionization bringing an adversarial faculty-administration relationship and contended that the threat of collective bargaining had already sent a "message" which had resulted in conciliatory gestures from the administration. Joining in opposition was the Undergraduate Student Government that passed overwhelmingly a resolution saying students would suffer from tensions between faculty and administration.

The vote on Feb. 11, 1994 was expected to be close, like that in 1979. This time, however, the faculty rejected collective bargaining decisively; with 84 percent of eligible faculty voting, the result was 258 in favor and 329 against. The reasons for the result were not entirely clear, but it reflected a national trend against collective bargaining, especially in higher education. In addition, local considerations worked to the advantage of opponents: the AAI was better organized than the fragmented opposition had been in 1979; a good deal of anecdotal evidence of problems resulting from collective bargaining at other Ohio universities, especially the University of Toledo, reinforced the AAI arguments; Olscamp's gestures to address some faculty concerns and his stated retirement plans reduced anti-administration sentiment.

However gratifying the outcome of the collective bargaining election was to the administration, that vote also marked the culmination of four years of persistent challenges, which had weakened Olscamp's capacity to lead. A loss of momentum likely would have occurred under any circumstances, for university presidents typically make their greatest marks during their first few years in office. "Olscamp fatigue" was

bound to occur. The board officially ignored the faculty evaluation, but it could not dismiss the faculty consensus of mediocre performance. Its members were cognizant that faculty and staff morale was low. Although the Board of Trustees continually gave him its support publicly, some members, as Olscamp wrote privately in 1991, were maneuvering to isolate him from some of its deliberations and to begin looking for his successor. It was difficult to discern when that would transition would take place. In 1991, Olscamp announced his plan to retire in June 1994. Then after his return from a three-month leave of absence in May 1992, the Board of Trustees, with the University facing one of its worst financial crises due to unexpected state budget cuts of $13 million over an 18-month period, extended his contract (with Platt abstaining) to June 30, 1996. Olscamp stated, "I feel I have an obligation … to continue during these difficult times." Once the budget situation stabilized, it was agreed that he would retire a year earlier. So this meant that the 1994-95 academic year would be devoted to the search for Olscamp's successor.

The contentious Olscamp years did transform the University. Since the change was grounded in established departments and was not dependent on ad hoc administrative structures, Olscamp was correct when he said in 1986 that it would be difficult to reverse his work.

The "new direction" was substantially achieved. The University strengthened its graduate program. The "mix" of undergraduate/graduate students fulfilled the expectations of the Role and Mission Statement. Between the fall of 1982 and fall of 1994, University enrollment increased modestly: from 18,038 to 18,906. The number of graduate students increased nearly 1,000, growing the graduate programs to nearly 18 percent of overall enrollment, compared to 13 percent previously. With the new doctoral programs, and the programs that had benefited from OBOR Selective Excellence funding flourishing, the "new direction" of 1982 was on course as Olscamp left office in 1995. ▪

Greek Life in the 1980s

Despite a weak national economy, Greek life in the '80s at BGSU experienced a "golden age." It was one of the top training grounds for aspiring Greek advisors, through the college student personnel graduate program, and was considered a leader for "best practices" across the country for Greek programming. Membership numbers reached a high of around 2,800 members with 25 fraternities and 17 sororities. Two sororities, Pi Beta Phi and Kappa Kappa Gamma, came on campus and one fraternity, Phi Sigma Kappa. Order of Omega, the national Greek leadership and scholarship honorary, was established in 1983. IFC and Panhellenic consistently won top regional awards, and there were more chapters winning awards from their respective national organizations than ever before. Major Greek movements, such as educational programming, Greek life research and evaluation, and anti-hazing initiatives, were led by BGSU Greek staff, graduate students and students. The Mid-America Interfraternity Council Association (MIFCA) was managed by BGSU staff and students from 1982 through the early 1990s. The ABC News show "20/20" recorded a segment at BGSU highlighting the Greek communities' anti-hazing programs.

The number of housemothers began to decline during this decade. Dr. Gerald Saddlemire, Professor Emeritus of college student personnel; Fayetta Paulsen, assistant vice president of student affairs/ residence life, and Greek director Wayne Colvin, recognized the need for an older adult presence and perspective in the Greek living units and created graduate scholarships that funded Greek graduate students as

Greek life in the '80s at BGSU experienced a "golden age."

replacements to housemothers. This attracted many former staff members of national and international fraternities and sororities. The first opposite-sex placements occurred in this decade when female graduate assistants were assigned to the Beta Theta Pi and Delta Upsilon fraternities in the same year. This practice was successful and continues today. Also, for the first time, a graduate student of color was placed in an all-white fraternity as unit director.

> Edward G. Whipple

1995-2008
The Premier Learning Community: The Ribeau Presidency

> One person familiar with the 1981-82 presidential search remarked afterward: "I don't think that any board will ever again be able to conduct a search in such secrecy."

Indeed by the time of the search for a successor to Paul Olscamp, the Board of Trustees regarded the earlier secrecy as a mistake, both procedurally and politically, and was committed to an open process. That was evident in the first communication to the University community from C. Ellen Connally, president of the Board of Trustees, who chaired the Presidential Search Committee. In contrast to the September 1981 message of Frazier Reams Jr. that his next communication would be to announce the new president, Connally in September 1994 invited faculty, staff and students to participate in an open forum with the search committee to offer suggestions on the desirable characteristics of the next president. That session was followed by periodic updates from the search committee on its progress. From the beginning, the search committee was committed to inviting finalists to

campus to address the University community and to meet various constituencies.

The "lessons" of the past were also evident in the unofficial criteria for the next president, which were intended to compensate for Olscamp's perceived shortcomings. Beyond the importance of a strong academic background and administrative experience, the 15-person Presidential Search Committee—which included five members of the Board of Trustees, four faculty, two students, and representatives of the alumni, staff and community—developed some less tangible priorities.[1] The overriding concern was finding a president with strong interpersonal skills who was committed to collegiality and who would cultivate support from groups on and off campus. Also given much prominence was fundraising; Bowling Green's endowment of some

---

1. The author was a member of the committee.

$45 million placed it seventh among the nine state universities in Ohio. The search committee developed a "leadership profile" that was based on prioritizing various "primary tasks" and "primary presidential attributes." The two leading tasks were "building collegial relationships with faculty, students and other constituencies" and "developing a 'shared vision' for the University." The primary attribute was "exhibiting strong social skills; i.e. be a 'people person.'" Significantly, in prioritizing the tasks there was little sentiment for "taking the University in a new direction" and strong opposition to "increasing undergraduate student enrollment." Indeed among the higher-rated tasks were essentially consolidating the changes of the Olscamp era: "to build upon the existing strengths of the University" and "to enhance the academic programs of BGSU." However, in its deliberations and early interaction with candidates, the search committee came to realize that the next president needed to rebuild the University's stature as an undergraduate institution. One candidate, who had considerable experience in higher education in Ohio, compared Bowling Green's image to "vanilla ice cream–bland, not offering anything exciting or innovative."

The search committee considered more than 150 candidates. Giving serious consideration only to incumbent presidents and chief academic officers, the committee by January 1995 narrowed the field to approximately 20 candidates, 16 of whom it met in off-campus interviews. From that group, the committee invited six for on-campus interviews that began on March 3 and concluded on March 28, 1995. The finalists were: Betty Turner Asher, president, University of South Dakota; David G. Carter, president, Eastern Connecticut State University; John R. Darling, chancellor, Louisiana State University at Shreveport; Lee B. Jones, executive vice president and provost, University of Nebraska System; Sidney A. Ribeau, vice president for academic affairs, California State Polytechnic University, and Sharon Wallace, vice president for academic affairs, North Dakota State University.

Each candidate spent two days on campus, beginning with an address to an open forum–all of which were well-attended–and meeting with vice presidents and other officials as well as various faculty, student, staff and community groups. The process was widely praised, and the open forums received considerable coverage in the *BG News*, the *Sentinel-Tribune* and *Toledo Blade*. Evaluation forms and other communications submitted to the committee indicated that while all the finalists had strong supporters as well as critics, the consensus clearly pointed to the emergence of Jones and Ribeau as the strongest candidates. The search committee shared that assessment. Accordingly, when it met jointly with all of the members of the Board of Trustees on March 30, the committee formally recommended Jones and Ribeau. The Board of Trustees invited Jones and Ribeau to return to campus for further discussions and then decided to offer the presidency to Ribeau. At a large campus gathering on Friday, April 14, 1995, the board's vice chair John Laskey introduced Sidney Ribeau as Bowling Green's ninth president.

Outgoing and personable with a good sense of humor, he was committed to incorporating faculty, staff and students into the governance process.

Ribeau, a 47-year-old native of Detroit, became Bowling Green's first African-American president. He left California where he was considered on a "fast-track" toward a presidency within that state's university system. After receiving his undergraduate degree at Wayne State University and his Ph.D. in communications at the University of Illinois, Ribeau taught at California State University, Los Angeles, where he began his administrative career as a department chair for three years and was credited with tripling the number of majors and rejuvenating the faculty. He then moved on to become dean of undergraduate studies at California State University at San Bernardino, a position that he held for three years before going to California Polytechnic University, San Luis Obispo, as dean of the college of liberal arts. After just two years as dean, he was named that university's vice president for academic affairs and he was in his third year in that office when he was named Bowling Green's president. A faculty member at California Polytechnic University said, "When he came

Sidney A. Ribeau was named president in 1995.

speaking—his enthusiasm and commitment always evident—to build consensus for his vision of the University. Asked early in his presidency what he stood for, Ribeau answered: "I'm philosophically passionate, intellectually curious.
I believe in the power of ideas; I believe in the life of the mind … I like to have fun, I like to work hard … I give 150 percent."

Like his predecessor, Ribeau was determined to be a transformative president, but he approached that mission differently. After being named president, Ribeau invited representatives of various groups and University leaders to tell him what faculty and staff expected when he addressed them at the beginning of the school year; an "inch-thick pile" of suggestions greeted him when he took office. He wanted to build change in ways that blended his priorities with the University community's concerns. As he later stated, "I made a conscious decision, right or wrong, to do the human capital side first. I just firmly believe that everything starts with people."

The initiatives of Ribeau's first months in office—the "building community" and "mission statement" projects—set the tone for his presidency. In his addresses to the University community at the beginning of the 1995 fall semester, Ribeau chose to speak on successive days to convocations of faculty/administrative staff and classified staff. Presidents had traditionally addressed faculty and high-ranking administrators as the highlight of the annual Opening Day program preceding the beginning of the school year; they had made presentations to the staff later in the semester. The symbolism of the change was significant, for it signaled Ribeau's determination to integrate the staff into the University's development. At both convocations, he drew spontaneous applause when he introduced a new management structure that emphasized cooperative, participatory planning—a "dynamic process where information flows in and out, rather than trickling down." Fundamental to Ribeau's vision of the University was fostering a sense of "community." The Faculty Senate, with Chair Fiona MacKinnon-Slaney who had served on the Presidential Search Committee, defined "building community" as its 1995-96 priority.

The University Task Force on Building Community, which Ribeau appointed in consultation with the senate leadership, had

here we know he wouldn't be here too long. He was too good to be just a vice president. It maybe happened a year or two earlier than we anticipated though." Ribeau's "fast-track" career, marked by four administrative positions in 11 years, led to some concern that his commitment to Bowling Green might be brief. One member of the Board of Trustees commented that he hoped for "five good years" from Ribeau. Few expected that he would equal Olscamp's 13-year tenure.

Ribeau embodied the attributes and priorities that governed the presidential search. Outgoing and personable with a good sense of humor, he was committed to incorporating faculty, staff and students into the governance process. His warm collegiality—the "leadership by charm" as one faculty member phrased it—did not mean that Ribeau lacked a determination to work assiduously for his objectives. Indeed he used his considerable skills in interpersonal relations and public wide-ranging charges: to promote a spirit of collaboration among faculty, staff and students; to evaluate the campus climate; to make recommendations for improving the work-life and study-life for all. During a campus meeting on Nov. 17, Ribeau invited all members of the University community to become participants in "change management." The broadly representative task force solicited input through an e-mail hotline, suggestion boxes and questionnaires. It sponsored "Focus on February"—a weeklong series of focus group/roundtable discussions centered on promoting a sense of common purpose. In the end the task force submitted a set of 19 "high-leverage" recommendations, including the clarification of the University mission, alignment of reward structures with University goals and forums to address "big picture" issues for all members of the University community. Many recommendations dealt specifically with improving interaction with students, particularly advising and "customer service." Important as the recommendations, most of which were implemented in some form, was the process itself that significantly enhanced the staff and student sense of stake in the University's mission. In sum, it provided a badly needed boost to morale.

"Building community" paralleled the formulation of a bold University mission statement. At the opening day convocation in August 1996, Ribeau began his second year by presenting the BGSU Vision Statement, which was based on the assumption that "we should be the best. If we set our sights on being good or only the best in northwest Ohio, then it doesn't give us the motivation to strive further." Developed from suggestions from individuals and groups over the previous year, the Vision Statement challenged the University community indeed to "be the best … to strive further" as it read:

    " *Bowling Green State University aspires to the premier learning community in Ohio and one of the best in the nation. Through the interdependence of teaching, learning, scholarship and service, we will create an academic environment grounded in intellectual discovery and guided by rational discourse and civility. Bowling Green State University serves the diverse and multicultural communities of Ohio, the United States and the world. "*

Ribeau stressed the importance of "rational discourse and civility" to promote the "greater good of the University." He set forth five "core values" to which all members of the University should adhere: "Respect for one another, cooperation, intellectual and spiritual growth, creative imaginings, and pride in a job well done." Anticipating a centerpiece of subsequent initiatives, he added: "It is totally unrealistic to expect students to leave with values that they aren't exposed to while they are here."

The initiatives of Ribeau's first year culminated in a festive presidential inauguration on Sept. 20, 1996—which turned into a celebration of community. The day-long event began with a formal program in the Lenhart Grand Ballroom in the University Union, which featured several speakers, including Elaine Hairston, chancellor of the Ohio Board of Regents, who praised Ribeau for "wisely call[ing] you to build community, to create the necessary relationship to position Bowling Green for success in the 21st century." The program embodied the community theme with comments from alumni, parents of students and from representatives of campus constituent groups, including faculty, administrative and classified staff, undergraduate and graduate students. The remarks of Pat Kitchen, chair of the Classified Staff Council, captured the enthusiasm of the occasion: "Last year our new president challenged us to become involved and to build community. With the assistance of President Ribeau, we have made a difference … [We are committed to] the highest standards of service, professionalism and innovation." The highlight of the inaugural was the ensuing "picnic with the prez" on the lawn in front of University Hall, where 8,000 students, faculty, staff and friends gathered for lunch, listened to music, danced and greeted the newly inaugurated president. To Charles Middleton, the recently appointed vice president for academic affairs, the event was "an incredible example of what we've all been talking about—this is community."

To realize the vision statement's objectives, Ribeau reorganized the administrative structure by centralizing considerable administrative authority in a resurrected provost office. "Our mission has changed to focus on the concept of a learning community," he told a reporter, "and our organizational structure has to reflect that."

Greek Life in the 1990s

Hazing reformation and the change in the drinking age in 1989 had huge impacts on the 1990s and resulted in defining, yet tumultuous times for the Greek community at BGSU. When the number of fraternities dropped to 20 and sororities declined to 16, the Greek membership on campus fell to around 2,000 by the end of the decade. Despite the losses in the overall number of groups, average chapter sizes remained similar to the levels experienced in the 1980s with fraternity memberships hovering in the mid-40s and sororities in the 90s. New groups continued to be attracted to BGSU during this decade including the fraternities Kappa Alpha Order and Delta Chi and sororities Sigma Kappa and the first Latina sorority, Sigma Lambda Gamma. Also, Tau Kappa Epsilon was re-established on campus.

Although the size of the community changed, the quality never wavered and many new initiatives begin. MIFCA evolved into the Mid-American Greek Council Association and continued to be managed by Greek staff and students for most of the decade. Greeks also brought the popular Dance Marathon to campus in 1995. Greek Odyssey, an orientation for new members, and Creating a Recreational Environment (C.A.R.E.), educational and fun programming, developed and evolved during this decade as well. Sorority recruitment was revamped in response to a national movement that included a shortened pledging period. The changes were first met with strong resistance, but were eventually welcomed and resulted in great recruitment success for the sororities. Greek unit directors completely replaced housemothers during this time period. Major events and memories from this time period included the Bessie the Cow at Sigma Phi Epsilon's Mudtug, Beta 500 (1998 marked its 35th anniversary), Delta Sigma Theta's Jabberwocky's, Delta Upsilon Bike Race, Fiji's, a ghost in the Chi Omega house, Greek Olympiad, Sigma Nu Car Stuff and Sigma Alpha Epsilon's Bed Races.

> *Edward G. Whipple*

Ribeau announced that the responsibilities of Middleton, who had been dean of Arts and Sciences at the University of Colorado, would be broadened to include the traditional responsibilities of provost. This step assured "the integration of the University's functions ... [which] emphasizes the centrality of our academic mission." Most University employees were engaged in the academic mission, and, Ribeau continued, "That's as it should be. Teaching, learning and research are what we do. We're not in business for sports; we're not in the business for new buildings. We're not in business for social events. We're in business for teaching and learning and the discovery of new knowledge." This reflected Ribeau's conviction that student affairs had to be integrated with academic programs. Under the reorganization, the vice presidents for student affairs and operations reported to the provost, not the president. Reporting to the president, in addition to the provost, were the vice president for planning and budgeting, a position to which Chris Dalton had been appointed in 1987 and would hold until 2006, and the vice president for external relations (formerly the vice president for University relations), a position filled by J. Douglas Smith in 1998 until his retirement in 2009.[2]

This administrative structure enabled Middleton during his three years as provost, to be the most powerful chief academic officer in University history. Working closely with Ribeau, Middleton was at the center of the important curricular, enrollment and retention initiatives. He provided leadership in redefining university policy on faculty evaluation, establishing a systematic program of evaluation of academic units, and, as a consequence of that review, addressing a number of problems in departments and colleges.

Ribeau's administrative style was best understood in the context of his commitment to being a "visible" leader and to bringing change. Whether in small or large groups, Ribeau was exceptionally effective in communicating his ideas and objectives, but, at the same time, "he did not have to be the center of attention." He was described as "self-confident without a trace of arrogance," and, with few exceptions, gained the loyalty of those with whom he worked. He established early a rapport with student leaders and met with student groups (he was fond of emphasizing how impressed he had been as a candidate with the "wisdom" of Bowling Green students when he learned that the *BG News* had endorsed him). He relied heavily on the provost and the vice presidents, soliciting their advice and delegating considerable authority. He avoided

---

2. Ribeau later established the positions of Executive Vice President (2000) and Vice President for Economic Development and Regional Growth (2006).

confrontations and showed disappointment or disagreement with subordinates "more by silence than by word." He acknowledged the prerogatives of the Faculty Senate, Board of Trustees and other groups, but in a sense kept them at arm's length. His reliance on special committees and task forces to consider his proposals, combined with his capacity to generate support for his goals, enabled him to marginalize his critics.

More important than administrative reorganization in marshalling resources for Bowling Green's new mission was the imperative of strengthening the faculty, whose numbers, especially at the senior ranks, had declined substantially. This was a result of the Early Retirement Incentive Program (ERIP) and Supplement Retirement Program (SRP), which had been instituted in 1989 to encourage early faculty retirements by purchasing service credit and offering three years of part-time post-retirement teaching. Justified as a means of reducing personnel costs as junior faculty replaced retirees and of heading off an anticipated nationwide surge of retirements in the mid-1990s, the financial and academic costs of ERIP/SRP had been controversial since their inception. A 1997 report found that since 1990 nearly half of the 734 full-time faculty had left the University (35-40 faculty opting for ERIP each year), and with the University relying heavily on temporary or part-time faculty (including those on the SRP) the number of full-time faculty had declined by 70 positions with an obvious detrimental effect on academic programs. Moreover, ERIP/SRP was costing about $7 million per year; just half of that expenditure would have enabled the University to hire 75 full-time assistant professors. Ribeau decided to end ERIP/SRP. He considered retirement incentives a mistake; he told the Board of Trustees, "We need to do more to make it attractive for faculty to stay." The board concurred and terminated ERIP/SRP at the end of the 1997-98 academic year. The following year the University began reinvesting in its permanent faculty, adding 67 new tenure-track positions, bringing the number of tenured/tenure-track faculty to 640.

The next task in building the "premier learning community" was addressing the problems of declining enrollment. In January 1997 at Ribeau's first State of the University speech, he focused on the decline in the enrollment and retention rate of first-year students over the previous five years. The University was running about 1,000 students below the state-mandated cap of 16,000 FTE (full-time equivalent) students, which meant that the FTE shortfall was costing about $10 million in state subsidy. Contributing to the enrollment problem was retention; between 1985-95, the first-to-second year retention dropped from 81.5 percent to 75.6 percent, while at peer institutions retention remained above 80 percent.

Speaking to University staff, Michael J. Marsh, a member of the Board of Trustees, expressed the prevailing view that the priorities of the Olscamp presidency had created the enrollment problem:

“ *It was deliberate on the part of the former administration to focus less on undergraduate education and more on research. I think the thinking was that would generate more money for the school, but it failed, and worse, we lost our niche … Ohio U. was more than happy to take that niche away from us and they have … We need to get back to selling undergraduate education because that's where the students are. The students are our life-blood.* ”

Among many recruitment efforts, the University found success using President's Day to bring prospective students to campus to visit classes and talk informally with University students, faculty and staff. Within a few years, students were citing the President's Day visits as one of the principal reasons for choosing Bowling Green.

Retention issues contributed to declining enrollment; between 1988 and 1997, the number of students in residence halls declined 25 percent–from 8,060 to 6,050–or a loss of nearly $5 million in revenue.

On the matter of retention, panels and interviews of students confirmed that the primary reason for leaving the University was a sense of alienation: "a lack of interaction, community and connection." Students spoke of impersonal and unrelated courses, a lack of classroom relevance to their aspirations and a sense of social isolation.

Against the background of the enrollment problem, Ribeau in the fall of 1997 proclaimed the need "to place the student at the heart of the learning community." To address sources of retention problems, the First Year Experience

Program, which had been established in 1996, undertook a concentrated effort to deal with the social and academic adjustment to college life, including substantial faculty and staff involvement in the process. Introduced in 1997 was *FYI* (*First Year Insight*), a 36-page publication sent to all new students in early August. When first-year students arrived on campus, about 50 members of the University community worked in residence halls to welcome them and their parents and to assist with the task of moving in. For the first time, the Student Union and Student Recreation Center were open on Move-In Weekend. A Faculty Night in residence halls provided an opportunity for students to meet with professors to discuss college courses, professorial expectations and studying techniques. Orientation of first-year students concluded with a New Student Convocation, which was followed by an All-Campus Picnic in front of University Hall.

First Year Experience undertook various initiatives including Freshman Interest Groups, ... Leaders in Residents, ... and Leading and Learning Together Teams ...

That fall also marked the beginning of Chapman Learning Center (CLC)—the University's first effort at bringing a broadly defined learning mission into a residential setting. "Learning communities" represented one of the prominent innovations in higher education to enhance the undergraduate academic experience, and they quickly became a signature feature of the Bowling Green curriculum. With 159 students and 10 faculty—recruited for their commitment to undergraduate teaching—as well as four upper class tutors, the CLC offered a core interdisciplinary liberal arts program with small classes, supplemented by communal cultural events.

In his opening day remarks in 1997, Ribeau also announced new awards that reinforced the teaching mission. The Presidential Academic Advising Award, to be presented annually by each college, was intended to "elevate academic advising in the eyes of the academic community." An Excellence in Teaching and Learning Award recognized faculty

members who engaged undergraduate and graduate students in the area of teaching and learning research. Conferring the title of Distinguished Teaching Professor on seven faculty members further reinforced the teaching mission. By 1997 Ralph Wolfe, English (1995); Edmund Danziger, history (1995); and Paul Haas, economics (1996) had been so recognized. Later in the Ribeau presidency, Stuart Keeley, psychology (2000); Janet Parks, human movement, sport and leisure studies (2002); Thomas Kinstle, chemistry (2004), and Sue Mota, legal studies (2007) joined their ranks.

Beyond the orientation programs, the First Year Experience office broadened its efforts to foster students' sense of belonging. New initiatives included a newsletter focused on first-year initiatives, plus three courses to ease transitional issues for new students. A new library position was established to meet the needs of first-year students by bringing information into freshman courses and residence halls. First Year Experience undertook various initiatives including Freshman Interest Groups which brought together groups of students who were taking the same two-or-three general education courses, Leaders in Residence which encouraged students to pursue leadership positions on campus, and Leading and Learning Together Teams which brought faculty and staff together with groups of students. A final significant undertaking was the BG Effect Monitoring Program, which matched 100 first-year students with faculty and staff members. These various endeavors relied substantially on integration of academic objectives with the Office of Student Affairs, which, after feeling "starved" during the Olscamp presidency, not only gained resources, but also played a prominent role in the broadly defined academic mission.

Of special importance to Ribeau was the President's Leadership Academy (PLA). Embodying the emphasis on building small communities and Ribeau's belief that Bowling Green graduates should possess value-driven leadership skills, the PLA had its origins in 1997 when Ribeau returned a $15,000 salary bonus to the University to establish a program to assist in the recruitment and development of students with leadership potential. The Board of Trustees established a $100,000 PLA scholarship endowment fund. Beginning in 1998 with an initial cohort of 21 students from the Toledo

Public Schools, the PLA, soon included students from across Ohio as well as several other states and Canada. By 2000 it could claim that its 70 students "comprise the most diverse group on campus, whether 'diversity' is measured by gender, racial/ethnic background, academics or social interests."

The recruitment efforts paid dividends. By 1998, Ribeau reported "extraordinary improvement" in freshman applications and envisioned first-year classes of 3,500 students within a few years. By the fall of 2000, the University enrolled 3,391 freshmen and the following year, it passed 3,500 with a class of 3,624. The growth of the freshman class and the improved retention were principal factors in the steady increase of the undergraduate enrollment by more than 1,000 students between 1996 and 2000. The quality of students, as measured by ACT scores and high school grades, also improved. The ending of early retirement incentives meant that by 2001, the full-time faculty (including those on temporary appointments) totaled 820, an increase of 140 over four years.

"Putting students first" and the various First Year Experience initiatives troubled some members of the faculty, who feared that such initiatives threatened academic standards. Representative of such concerns was an essay, "Suppose We Really Cared About Freshmen" written by two Distinguished Teaching Professors—M. Neil Browne of Economics and Stuart Keeley of Psychology—which was published in *The Monitor* in 1999. "Buttons, banners and cheerleading sessions heralding our concern for freshmen," they wrote, "are hollow substitutes for the incredibly difficult work of caring [which] distinguish[es] between caring that responds to the current expressions of desire by freshmen and those that respond to their reflective, long-term needs." The former led to "enabling" teaching, which treated students as "spun glass

President Ribeau established the President's Leadership Academy in 1997.

... too brittle to experience frustration, criticism, or failure ... giving lots of credit for sloppy work ... affirming the quality of any and all student comments ... [and] being repeatedly tolerant of late papers, forgotten assignments and class absences." Such behavior might develop an institutional image as "caring," but "if we really care about freshmen, we will have the courage to turn a deaf ear to certain of their inclinations, while assisting them to appreciate the compassion and insight implicit in that expression of care."

The extent to which innovative measures ran such risks not withstanding, few questioned Ribeau's assertion that CLC was a "phenomenal success" which served as a model for the development of additional "residential learning" or "themed" communities (the latter house students with common interests and hold community events, but do not include any special curriculum). By 2000-01, the University had established several residential communities including the Natural and Health Sciences Residential Community, international housing, music housing, La Maison Francais and Honors Program housing (the latter two pre-dated the "residential community" emphasis). A task force in 2001 recommended the development of additional residential learning options that would enable every student to participate in a learning community. The "learning community" option, however, seemed to have limited appeal to undergraduates. None of the

The Students Speak: The Bowen-Thompson Student Union

Students took the initiative in pressing for a new student union. In the fall of 1994, the presidents of the United Student Government and Graduate Student Senate met with Edward G. Whipple, the newly appointed Vice President for Student Affairs, regarding the poor condition of the University Union and the need for major renovation or a new structure. When presidential candidates were interviewed on campus in March 2005, students stressed their concerns about the Union.

So it was not surprising that Ribeau, in his first address as president, identified the "new or larger union" as a "hot spot issue." Ribeau supported Whipple's recommendation that a Student Union Needs Analysis and Feasibility Study be undertaken and, as part of his administrative reorganization, Ribeau shifted responsibility for the Union from the Operations area to Student Affairs. By December 1996, the feasibility study put forth three alternatives: building a new union located elsewhere on campus, constructing an addition to the Student Services Building, expanding and renovating the existing Union—which was judged to be the most feasible. The University Architect presented a plan, which increased the size of the union from 117,000 to 207,000 square feet and required the demolition of Prout Hall; its cost was $34 million.

The plans encountered opposition from students living in Prout Hall, who organized a campaign to save their residence hall, circulating petitions and sending representatives to a Board of Trustees meeting in December 1997.

The project, however, went ahead with the Board of Trustees issuing bonds to cover most of the cost, but with plans of "raising a significant amount from private sources"—set at $6 million. In December 1999, the University Union of forty years was closed and construction/renovation began. A year later Ribeau announced that Robert and Ellen (Bowen) Thompson, both Bowling Green graduates in the 1950s, were contributing $3,000,000, which put the campaign over the $6 million target, with private funding reaching eventually $6.7 million.

In January 2002, a celebration marked the opening of the Bowen-Thompson Student Union, with its expanded food service facilities and meeting rooms, and housing as well a theatre, bookstore, galleries, post office and Student Affairs offices. The Lenhart Ballroom was preserved. The Bowen-Thompson Student Union became a center of campus life, more than fulfilling the dreams of those student leaders who saw the need for an enlarged and "student-centered" union.

Fireworks capped off the opening of the renovated student union, with a new name and a lot of new spaces and amenities.

learning communities was operating at capacity. Proponents believed that a better understanding of the communities and a wider range of choices would recruit more students. Additional residential learning communities were thus established, including the Arts Village, Global Village, IMPACT (Integrating Moral Principles and Critical Thinking–offered to honors students), La Communidad for students interested in the Spanish language and culture, and Partners in Context and Community for students interested in teaching in high-need urban schools. This meant that by 2008-09, nine residential learning communities were in place. In addition, there were five designated residential "theme communities" (Greek housing, Army ROTC, aviation, Batchelder music and wellness).

The capstone of the reorientation of the undergraduate mission was the focus on values. In his March 1, 2001 State of the University Address – "Big Questions, Worthy Dreams: Creating A Principled Community"–Ribeau stated, "We need to place the University in the central role of ethical leadership. We have an opportunity to re-establish our roles as leaders–not as responders, not as reactors, but as leaders." He went on to say that there was no gain turning out graduates who lack moral responsibility. Through its programs–and most importantly through its faculty, administrators and staff as models–the University needed to teach students to put social purpose ahead of self-interest.

Ribeau regarded this as a critical step. When asked later asked what he regarded as his most important accomplishment, he replied:

" Our first-year program we started for new students. We've developed an innovative approach to creating a student-centered learning community in which values, civic engagement and character development are central. We also appointed a task force of respected faculty, staff and administrators and asked them to develop a plan to integrate values exploration, critical thinking, civic engagement and character development throughout the curricular and co-curricular experience. This program developed into the BGeXperience (BGX) and is highly successful. It is a signature program that has received national attention. "

In 2000 Ribeau, had appointed a University Committee on Vision and Values (UCVV). Its charge was to examine the role of general education in the development of ethnically aware, civic-minded students, and to consider "how we can best integrate values exploration, critical thinking, character development and civic responsibility throughout the entire academic and co-curricular experience." Behind this initiative was Ribeau's conviction that rational discourse was desperately needed in American society.

The UCVV, which was chaired by Donald Nieman, dean of the College of Arts and Sciences, faced as challenging a mission as any committee in the University's history: Could the entire university be engaged in an exploration of values? Would faculty accept this mission? In the senate and elsewhere, skeptical faculty asked, "Should the University be "teaching" values? Whose values would be taught? Why not teach ethics rather than 'values' which carried certain political connotations?"

Others raised objections to "top-down" curricular reform: "Should not faculty be the source of change?" Mindful of these questions, the UCVV undertook considerable research on values education and pedagogy. In the end, it recommended a program with the objective of "critical thinking about values" and reliance on modestly restructured general education courses. Specifically, by linking first-year orientation to a required first-semester, 25-student general education course with a values component, the University would communicate its priorities and expectations from the moment that students arrived. The UCVV also recommended co-curricular activities, as well as upper level experiences and additional courses to provide coherence to the values emphasis, but the first-year experience was the most critical step and where the program has been centered. Thus, when the UCVV submitted its report in May 2001, it recommended creating BGX, making "critical thinking about values" the unifying theme of the undergraduate curriculum. Nieman contended, quite reasonably, that while the initiative was "top-down," the implementation was "bottom-up" reflecting considerable faculty input.

In the fall of 2002, the recommendations were tested in a pilot project involving 123 entering freshmen. Following a four-day orientation, they

The First Year Experience Program, which included the BG Experience, was designed to ease students' transitions to college.

enrolled in one of five small general education courses with a values component, which included a staff member and an upper-class student mentor in addition to the faculty member. The diversity of offerings (American culture studies, philosophy, biology, business administration and popular culture) fulfilled an important curricular point of the UCVV and its successor, the University Committee on Values and the BG Experience (UCVBG): that values issues could be incorporated into established general education courses across a range of disciplines. Sensitive to faculty concerns about "teaching values," the UCVBG, in its report to the Board of Trustees in February 2002, stated emphatically: "If we are serious about making values central to the Bowling Green experience, our focus must be on critical thinking about values and *not* on prescribing the values students should embrace."

In addition to the criticisms of the "top-down" nature of the values initiative, some faculty and others argued the need for a coherent strategy that would integrate curricular changes with the vision statement. Clearly the goal and mission statement of 1984 was no longer relevant. In 2002 Ribeau and Provost John Folkins, who had been appointed to that office two years earlier and was committed to building a consensus in support of BGX and a redefined mission, named an Academic Planning Team, headed by Milt Hakel

(psychology). Following extensive discussions and review of University objectives and resources, it submitted the University Academic Plan, which centered on the themes of inquiry, engagement and achievement inside and outside the classroom as key to becoming the "premier learning community." To its credit, the Academic Planning Team insisted on continuing discussions and on assessment—a 2006 Progress Report that related indicators of student, faculty, curricular and enrollment progress to the objectives of the academic plan.

Bowling Green's commitment to the values initiative received national attention. To some figures in higher education, Ribeau's effort heralded a return to an earlier generation of university presidents who addressed public issues. In an article in the *Chronicle of Higher Education*, the former president of Notre Dame University, Theodore Hesburgh who represented the public intellectual, lamented that university presidents, absorbed in internal operations and averse to risk-taking, no longer spoke out on values, issues and policy. Hesburgh's comments led Jon Dalton, director of the Center for Student Values of Florida State University to write: "One university president who has played a very public leadership role in addressing moral and civic learning is Sidney Ribeau." Ribeau spoke widely and enthusiastically about BGX. He frequently mentioned the wasted opportunity if universities produced graduates with high grades but who lacked a sense of civic responsibility. He insisted that the emphasis needed to be on academic-based "self-reflection and self-exploration [that] helps students answer a core question: 'what is important to you?'"

BGX attracted considerable private support. Three important contributions in 2004 were instrumental in broadening the program. Sky Bank, on the occasion of the retirement of Edward Reiter as the senior chairman of Sky Financial Group, provided a $500,000 contribution for the creation of the Sky Bank - Edward and Linda Reiter Endowed Lectureship: Values and Ethics in the Workplace. The Reiters had earlier contributed $250,000 for the BGX program. In addition, Hugh Smith, a 1953 graduate, and his wife, Barbara Smith, pledged $1 million in cash and deferred gifts, and Ronald Whitehouse, a 1967 graduate, and his wife Carol Sue (Lee) Whitehouse, who also attended BGSU, designated $150,000 to BGX (as part of a $1 million gift).

These contributions were vital to the dramatic expansion of BGX to include all entering freshmen in the fall of 2005 – a commitment of resources to "investing in student success by providing 3,650 first-year students with the opportunities of a major university in a very personal, small college atmosphere." To provide 150 BGX classes of 25 students was a remarkably ambitious undertaking. The University, which placed a premium on fostering first-year student connections with faculty and mentors, was committed to having classes taught by tenured or tenure-track faculty and to recruiting outstanding upperclassmen as peer mentors. To direct the program, the University appointed George Agich, who was the F. J. O'Neill Chair in Clinical Bioethics at the Cleveland Clinic Lerner College of Medicine of Case Western University; since 1997 he had also served as an adjunct professor in Bowling Green's philosophy department,

For three days before the beginning of the fall semester in August 2005, entering students participated in a BGX introduction – an orientation program comprised of small groups dealing with substantial intellectual content. Under the leadership of a student mentor and the course's professor, students began the exploration of values by discussing a common reading (The

Kite Rider). Following the BGX Introduction which ended with all freshmen participating in a Sunday convocation, each orientation group continued in its respective Fall Semester BGX class that began the next day with the same professor and peer mentor.

The launching of the BGX program paralleled Ribeau's final initiative: the Scholarship of Engagement. This effort drew upon his long-standing commitment to having the University play a prominent role in dealing with regional issues, but it was given impetus by pressures from Columbus to demonstrate that higher education could address economic and social problems. Early in his presidency, Ribeau had established Partnerships for Community Action (PCA), which under the direction of Kathy Farber became a center of outreach cooperative programs; this was followed in 1999 by the Center for Innovative and Transformative Education (CITE), which under Bill Armaline focused on collaborations for school reform. Supported by substantial grants from the U.S. Department of Education, BGSU, in cooperation with two partner institutions (Western Michigan University and the University of Illinois-Chicago) formed a Midwest Educational Reform Consortium that worked with schools in low-income areas to improve student performance; Bowling Green cooperated with the Toledo Public Schools.

In the fall of 2004, Ribeau launched the Organizing for Engagement Initiative. He pressed for relating faculty research and scholarship to the engagement mandate, but as a task force reported, few disciplines lent themselves to such scholarship and, even in those cases, a better use of faculty expertise often was to work with local groups or agencies in consulting capacities rather than through research projects.

By the time that BGX was launched, the initiatives of the previous decade were yielding impressive results. Instrumental in attracting students was the doubling of commitment to institutional financial assistance and scholarships between 1999 and 2004; a number of scholarships were expanded or added, including: the merit-based scholarship program, the Falcon Soars Scholarship, the Orange and Brown Scholarship Grants, the Faculty Achievement Scholarship, University Professors Scholarships and the Michigan Success Scholarships. These enabled the

University to compete for promising students. The entering classes of the fall of 2004 and 2005 were the largest in the University's history (3,800 and 3,650 respectively), but also included the highest percentages of students with ACT scores over 30 and students of color (17 percent). The enrollment surge meant that for the first time since the post-World War II student boom, the University was unable to meet the demand for on-campus living, and had to lease nearby off-campus apartments to accommodate the overflow.

The undergraduate initiatives earned the University considerable favorable attention. Beginning in 2003, the *U.S.News and World Report* (*USNWR*) in its annual "America's Best Colleges" edition listed Bowling Green among its "programs to look for," citing the first-year experience programs, BGX and the learning communities as "outstanding examples of academic programs believed to lead to student success." The Chapman Learning Program gained national visibility and the book *Creating Learning Communities* (2000), presented CLC as a model for other universities; the authors praised Chapman for its "bottom-up" origins and for its reliance on senior faculty.

In 2007, three major national organizations recognized Bowling Green's undergraduate curriculum. The Carnegie Foundation for the Advancement of Teaching cited Bowling Green's curricular engagement—only one of five colleges and universities to be honored, and the only large university so recognized. The Association

of American Colleges and Universities cited BGX as one of the few programs nationwide that was noted for demonstrating that "principles in practice fostered civic, intercultural and ethical learning." Finally, the Council for Higher Education Accreditation selected Bowling Green as the recipient of its annual Award for Institutional Progress in Student Learning Outcomes. Its president Judith Eaton stated, "Bowling Green serves as a solid example of the enormous progress that institutions are making through the implementation of comprehensive thoughtful and effective initiatives."

In 2009-10 Bowling Green was cited again by the magazine's special report for its first-year experience programs (one of 30 schools so recognized) and learning communities (one of 26), and now in a distinctive third category as well: "a strong commitment to teaching," Among 80 "national universities" singled out "for their unusual commitment to undergraduate teaching and to emphasizing that aspect of academic life," Bowling Green was ranked 11th (tied with Rice University, University of California-Berkeley, University of Chicago, University of Michigan, University of North Carolina).

Student life was directly affected in many ways by the curricular changes. The integration of the academic mission with student affairs blurred some of the distinctions between the "academic" and "student" sides of campus life. Students were notably active in promoting the movement for a new student union. Fraternities and sororities proved resilient and innovative during some difficult times.

In one important aspect of student social life, the University was actively engaged in influencing behavior. Student drinking became a matter of concern because of the change in the legal drinking age in Ohio and evidence of an increase in "binge drinking" at colleges and universities across the country. The University undertook nationally recognized initiatives to address the problem of alcohol abuse. The research of Terry Rentner of the journalism faculty played a prominent role in this endeavor. Her surveys of undergraduate students found that about 80 percent consumed alcohol and of those 50-60 percent indulged in "binge drinking" and had engaged in some form of public misconduct.

BGSU has been cited consistently by U.S.News and World Report, first in 2003 for its first-year experience programs and most recently for its strong commitment to teaching.

Women's Basketball's Greatest Moment: The Sweet Sixteen Season, 2006–07

Curt Miller, who became women's basketball coach in 2001-02, rebuilt the Falcons into the dominant team in the MAC. They won MAC championships three consecutive years, beginning in 2004-05. In each of the first two seasons, Bowling Green lost opening round NCAA games, to Kansas and UCLA respectively. Then came the magic 2006-07 season.

In the NCAA regionals held at East Lansing, Michigan, the seventh-seeded Falcons got by 10th-seed Oklahoma State, 70-66. This set the stage for a match with second-seeded Vanderbilt. With a few thousand fans that made the 135-mile journey from Bowling Green cheering them on, the Falcons upset the Commodores, 59-56. "It's the biggest win in program history for our conference, for our school, for our community," Miller said afterward, as Bowling Green became the first MAC women's team to reach the Sweet 16 Round. A loss to Arizona State ended the season–with an overall record of 31 wins and 4 losses.

The team made a triumphant return to campus. Ali Mann, the MAC co-player of the year, described the reception: "You can't put into words how awesome it was. The welcome that we got when we came back from the Sweet 16 was incredible. Everyone knew us. We went over to the Dance Marathon, and all the students there were just going crazy for us. We felt like we were rock stars."

First-year students, athletes and fraternity/sorority members were found to be the most vulnerable. Convinced from her research that the traditional reliance on lectures about alcohol and drug abuse was not working, Rentner, through a grant from the Ohio Department of Alcohol and Drug Addiction Services, began a program in 1997 that took leaders into residence halls and Greek houses to conduct focus group discussions. As one part of the alcohol prevention programs administered through the Wellness Connection, this effort sought to dispel the traditional belief that drinking was necessary to "fit-in." As evidence indicated that "binge drinking" was declining, the Bowling Green program attracted attention. The U.S. Department of Education listed the initiative among the six best in the nation and awarded the University a $75,000 grant to extend the program into high schools, which was vital, for, as Rentner found, "the problem begins before the student arrives." The University received the 2003 Exemplary Prevention Program Award from the Ohio Department of Alcohol and Drug Addiction Services. A year later it was among the 10 universities to receive a National Collegiate Alcohol Awareness Week Award. And in 2005, the Department of Education awarded the University a two-year $300,000 grant to fund an alcohol education program for high-risk students.

Among the more important changes in student life were in student media and intercollegiate athletics. BG 24 News was started in 1992 by two students, Chris Hursh and Bob Jones, and became the local television news source, airing on campus and over the local cable system. In 2007, the city of Bowling Green suddenly found itself without a live morning news radio program when WFOB-FM, based in Fostoria, discontinued its broadcast from Bowling Green. A cooperative venture involving the Bowling Green Chamber of Commerce, the longtime local broadcaster Dave Horger and the University led to a weekday morning broadcast carried by WBGU-FM 88. Ewart Skinner, chair of the telecommunications department, said that this opportunity fulfilled "our goal … to bring the station closer to the community and to maintain professionally oriented community-engaged student leadership of the organization." The following year, 1610 AM-WFAL changed to a web-focused medium of transmission known as WFAL "Falcon Radio" accessed on the web as well as on cable television.

The rapid changes in communications technology were also reflected in the print media. The *BG News* began an all-digital production process, followed by the other print publications including *The Gavel*, *The Key* and *The Obsidian*. *The Key*, matching trends on other college campuses, ceased publication as a yearbook in 2008 and was converted to a magazine format. A new companion website of *The BG News* was launched in 2001 and evolved into an interactive community Web portal, bgviews.com. The sweeping changes in readership and advertising, affecting commercial newspapers between 2005-10, also began impacting

Firelands College: An Expanding Mission

Since commemorating its 25th anniversary in 1993-94, Firelands College continued to expand its regional mission. Beginning in 2000-01, enrollment steadily increased; the fall semester head-count, which had dropped to 1,233 in 1999, surpassed 2,000 in 2005 and reached 2,284 in 2008.

Improved facilities and a broadened curriculum were instrumental. In 2003, the Cedar Point Center—the first new building on campus since 1972 opened with private fund-raising accounting for $2.7 million of the $8 million cost; Cedar Point Inc. contributed $1million. The facility features fiber-optic and wireless technologies for its classrooms and conference facilities, and distance-learning technologies that have facilitated main campus/Firelands instruction. With many Firelands students "place-bound" and unable to complete degrees on campus, Firelands has been authorized to offer selected baccalaureate degrees, including Liberal Studies, Applied Health Science, Early Childhood Education, Criminal Justice, Technology and General Business Administration.

Throughout its history, BGSU Firelands and Firelands students have benefited by generous support of local benefactors, including BGSU alumnus George L. Mylander of Sandusky through his Mylander Foundation Scholarships.

The $8 million Cedar Point Center features state-of-the-art technologies for classrooms and conference facilities.

print publishing at universities across the country. The University's Student Publications was forced to change its operating structure during the 2009-10 academic year to manage decreased print advertising revenues.

Intercollegiate athletics underwent a significant transformation as a result of the Title IX requirement that university expenditures on men's and women's athletic teams had to approximate the percentage of male and female undergraduate students. At Bowling Green as elsewhere, this led to the development of more intercollegiate sports for women and to the elimination of some men's programs. The high cost of football and hockey left "nonrevenue" men's sports vulnerable. Wrestling and lacrosse were eliminated earlier, and then in 2002 four more men's teams—swimming, tennis and indoor and outdoor track—were dropped to bring the University closer to Title IX compliance. Each of these sports had strong traditions, and their loss was keenly felt. For instance, the lacrosse program, started in 1966 under coach Mickey Cochrane, had become a national power, going to the NCAA tournament in 1972 and 1973. When 50 alumni of the lacrosse team gathered in the fall of 2009, disappointment lingered. Matthew Kenny, class of 1976, said "It breaks our hearts … There was a lot of real sadness and people were angry." Jim Plaunt, class of 1966, who played on the first team, said "This is very bittersweet … It was a great program and if they had the foresight to carry it on it would have been self-supporting by now. … All these guys here—they would have supported this program forever."

However regrettable such losses, intercollegiate athletics became far more representative of the student body. The long-standing vibrant women's sports program moved from the periphery of athletics to become part of a fully integrated intercollegiate athletic program. The emergence of women's basketball to national prominence has been the most visible aspect of the transformation, but that ought not to obscure the fact that by its centennial, Bowling Green women athletes were competing in nine other sports: cross-country, track, swimming, soccer, volleyball, golf, softball, tennis and gymnastics. Men's sports—in addition to football, hockey and basketball—now include golf, soccer, cross-country and baseball. The reinvigorated athletic program has produced a few successful coaches, whose lengthy careers suggest that not all "legendary coaches" are in Bowling Green's past. Two longtime coaches reached the 500-win milestone in 2009: baseball coach Danny Schmitz, who completed his 19th season with a second consecutive regular season MAC championship and who earlier led the Falcons to two MAC tournament titles; volleyball coach Denise Van De Walle in her 27th season, which includes three regular season MAC titles and one MAC tournament championship.

The success of women's basketball brought national recognition and a devoted fan base. Average attendance at Anderson Arena for women's games increased from 647 in 2000-01 to 1,763 in 2008-09. Men's basketball, while having several strong seasons including twice earning the best overall regular season record in the MAC, never advanced beyond the semi-finals of the MAC tournament. The football team went to four bowl games in the new century, winning two and losing two.

... Ribeau confronted a challenge to some of the University's doctoral programs, which resulted from an Ohio Board of Regents ... review of programs in selected disciplines.

Like the students and staff, faculty were affected by the changes of the Ribeau presidency. Ribeau's emphasis on the undergraduate mission lessened some of the visibility given research and graduate programs during the Olscamp era. Faculty, however, became more research-oriented than ever, owing in part to the redefinition of criteria for faculty tenure and promotion, completed in 1998 under Charles Middleton as provost, which placed a clearer university-wide emphasis on research and creative activity than had been true in previous personnel policy. This meant that the younger faculty, many of whom were hired after the termination of the early retirement program, started their careers with a stronger research commitment than had their predecessors. Ribeau, who was sensitive of criticism that he lacked commitment to

the research mission, frequently spoke of its importance. In 1997 he established the Innovative Basic Research Award to recognize faculty scholarship; on that occasion he said: "I do not want anyone to think we do not highly prize what we do in the area of research ... The discovery of new knowledge today can be the solution to a societal problem tomorrow or the next day."

Recognition of scholarly accomplishments, however, seemed less significant.

The naming of the recipient of the annual Olscamp Research Award—the University's most prestigious recognition of faculty scholarship—was moved from the general Faculty Recognition Dinner to a Research Conference. The practice, initiated by Hollis Moore and continued by Paul Olscamp, of holding convocations for the formal conferral of Distinguished Research/Artist Professorships ended. Nonetheless, during the Ribeau presidency, the Board of Trustees conferred that title on five faculty: John Sampen in music performance studies (1996), Marilyn Shrude in musicology and composition (2001) and Thomas Muir in art (2005) were named Distinguished Artist Professors; and Peggy Giordano in sociology (2000) and Verner Bingman in psychology (2008) were appointed Distinguished Research Professors. In addition, the resignation of one of the three Ohio Eminent Scholars led to the appointment of Peter Lu, an internationally recognized expert in the field of single-molecule spectroscopy, as a second Photochemical Sciences Eminent Scholar.

What remained intact was the University's commitment to a few focused doctoral programs of quality. Early in his administration, Ribeau confronted a challenge to some of the University's doctoral programs, which resulted from an Ohio Board of Regents (OBOR) review of programs in selected disciplines. It was a confusing process, aptly described by Louis Katzner, vice provost for research and dean of the graduate college, as "a mindless attempt to do something without putting all the cards on the table."

In any event, five Bowling Green programs—psychology, English, history, education administration and biological sciences—were subject to review. Psychology sailed through, but the others encountered some problems. The Board of Regents curtailed funding for the literature part of the doctoral program in English (ironically, the major strength of the University's first doctoral program 35 years earlier) in favor of emphasizing the rhetoric area—a decision that the University accepted. Along with five of the seven other doctoral programs in history, OBOR ended Bowling Green's subsidy. When biological sciences was similarly threatened, the department and University—with Ribeau playing a prominent role—marshaled considerable support from alumni and other sources, while also addressing the Regents' concerns about aspects of the program; the doctorate was preserved. The Ph.D. in educational administration had in the previous five years developed a second area of concentration in higher education administration, which built on the strength of the master's level program in college student personnel. The OBOR review resulted in changing the program for public school administrators to a Doctor of Education degree, with the Ph.D. program concentrated in higher education administration.

With respect to the history program, Ribeau and the Board of Trustees decided to continue it despite the lack of state subsidy; it was maintained that the program's concentration on policy history and its strong record of placing graduates justified this unprecedented arrangement. Bowling Green's initiative in this regard, however, was not unique; presidents at the five other institutions similarly affected continued doctoral programs in history despite the Board of Regents' action.

After several years of planning, the University added the Doctor of Musical Arts. Like other doctoral programs, it concentrated on an area of strength: in this case, contemporary music. The Doctor of Musical Arts built on a strong master's program of about 100 students; moreover, since 1980 the College of Musical Arts had hosted the New Music and Arts Festival, and, with an Academic Challenge grant, had created in 1990 the Mid American Center for Contemporary Music. In May 2005, OBOR approved the University's first new doctorate in a decade.

Several faculty initiatives gave the University prominence in international education, especially in programs that promoted democracy, which became an important priority of American foreign policy. Working with a group of colleagues in the College of Education and Human Development, Alden Craddock (teaching and learning) spearheaded a number of initiatives, including

grants from the U.S. Department of Education to further civic education in South Africa, Poland and the Ukraine, and from the U.S. Agency for International Development to work with educators in Lebanon and Morocco in developing democratic citizenship curricula for schools and universities. Patricia Kubow (leadership and policy studies) was recognized at the White House in 2002 for her role in democratic education in the former Soviet Union and Africa. A subsequent Department of State grant enabled Kubow to continue her work on the culture of democracy in South Africa and Kenya. Still another initiative was a two-year grant from 2005-07 under the Department of State Middle East Partnership Initiative awarded to Laura Lengel (interpersonal communications) and Catherine Cassara-Jemai (journalism) to work with university faculty and students in Tunisia as part of a program to train journalists in societies moving toward democracy.

After a decade of falling behind in fundraising, the University worked to rebuild neglected relationships and expand the scope of fundraising ...

The graduate programs in chemistry and sociology were enhanced by the development of research centers during the first decade of the millennium. The Center for Photochemical Sciences received in excess of $4 million from the state's Third Frontier and Innovation Incentive Awards, as well from federal and private support of research, thus enhancing its reputation as a leading research center.

With funding from the National Institutes of Health, faculty in the sociology department established the Center for Family and Demographic Research. One of only 15 centers of its kind in the United States, the center was enhanced by research grants to its participating faculty between 2004-07 totaling more than $2 million and a second NIH grant in 2007 of $1.3 million. In 2008 the first-ever National Center for Marriage Research was established, supported by a U.S. Department of Health and Human Services grant of $4.35 million over five years. Modeled on the National Poverty Research Center, which had a major impact on governmental policy, the National Center for Marriage Research, like the Center for Family and Demographic Research, addresses an important area of public policy.

In the College of Business Administration, a gift of $1.5 million from Bill Dallas, a 1977 graduate, matched by a $1.5 million gift from the Pioneer Fund in recognition of Olympic gold medal figure skater and Bowling Green native, Scott Hamilton, established the Dallas-Hamilton Center for Entrepreneurial Leadership and endowed the Ernest and Dorothy Hamilton Professorship of Entrepreneurship honoring Hamilton's late parents, both of whom were University faculty. The entrepreneurship program also received $250,000 from Patrick L. and Debra (Scheetz) Ryan, both 1974 graduates. As a result of gifts establishing the Maurer Family Professorship, William J. and Mary Catherine Primrose Professorship and the James R. Good Chair of Global Strategy, the College of Business Administration had by the University's centennial seven endowed professorships, including the earlier Ashel Bryan/Huntington Bank Professorship, Ernst & Young Professorship of Accountancy and the Owens-Illinois Professorship.

The departments of biological sciences and mathematics and statistics benefited from major alumni gifts, which brought three endowed professorships. In addition to the entrepreneurship donation, Patrick L. and Debra (Scheetz) Ryan endowed a professorship in biological sciences with gifts totaling $500,000. In 2005, a $2 million trust given by Jean Pasakarnis Buchanan, a 1952 graduate who had recently retired from Massachusetts General Hospital, was designated to support a visiting professorship, scholarships and an electronic learning center. As part of a $1 million contribution from James Bailey, class of 1967, and his family, $500,000 was designated for an endowed professorship in mathematics, a way of acknowledging, in Bailey's words, his indebtedness to the late Cliff Long "a great math professor who made all the difference in the world."

J. Robert Sebo, class of 1958, made a $4.9 million gift to fund principally the Sebo Athletic Center at the north end of Doyt Perry Stadium, but also to support the Sebo Entrepreneurship Lecture Series and to enhance the jazz program in the College of Musical Arts.

SEBO ATHLETIC CENTER

After a decade of falling behind in fundraising, the University worked to rebuild neglected relationships and expand the scope of fundraising under the leadership of J. Douglas Smith, vice president for University advancement, and Marcia Sloan Latta, senior associate vice president and director of alumni and development. The BGSU Foundation Board grew beyond Ohio and Michigan into a national group, whose members contributed to the University and were actively engaged in fund-raising.

Ribeau understood the psychology of giving. His emphasis on students and the values initiative played very well with the donors. As Smith phrased it, Ribeau was "powerful and effective in framing the University's mission and the importance of private support to achieve that goal."

BGSU Trustee J. Robert Sebo made a $4.9 million gift to fund the Sebo Athletic Center, and support an entrepreneurship lecture and the jazz studies program in the College of Musical Arts.

The first major campaign since the 75th anniversary—the Student Success Initiative launched in 1998-99—was a "trial run" of fundraising potential. Under Latta's leadership, the campaign raised more than $18 mission in two years to support the Cedar Point Center at Firelands, the Bowen-Thompson Student Union and scholarships.

Buoyed by that success, the steering committee for the centennial campaign—Building Dreams, which was launched in 2002—set its sights high. The steering committee, co-chaired by Kermit Stroh and Ronald Whitehouse and with Latta as campaign director, rejected a consulting firm's feasibility study that suggested a $60 million goal, and instead worked to raise $120 million.

Whether Ribeau's initiatives will survive depends on imponderables—future leadership, economic conditions, decisions in Columbus ...

By the time that the Building Dreams campaign was gaining momentum, Ribeau seemed to lose some of the zest that had characterized his leadership for more than a decade. His commitment to Bowling Green had always been strong. He had rejected presidential overtures from several other universities and had talked about wanting to "see things through" at Bowling Green and to help celebrate its Centennial. Indeed his contract ran through 2012.

Yet, in the judgment of several faculty and administrators, Ribeau missed an opportunity to consolidate his achievements. In the past some of those who worked with him had been troubled by his "big picture" emphasis and seeming inattention to the details of implementing change. The early success of BGX would have benefited from wider publicity as a unique enterprise both in its objectives and its pedagogy for a university of Bowling Green's size. Instead, Ribeau allowed some of its essential components—the orientation program and the commitment to regular faculty as instructors—to be scaled back. Moreover, the enrollment and retention momentum was losing ground. Expectations of first-year classes continuing in the range of 3,750 were not realized; the sizes of the classes of 2006 and 2007 were

disappointing, falling to 3,026 in the latter year. The decline was attributed to reductions in financial assistance. In any event, main campus enrollments peaked at 19,108 in the fall of 2006 (reflecting the large freshman classes of 2003-05) and then began a steady decline, beginning with nearly 400 fewer students in the fall of 2007. The graduate enrollment remained level at about 3,000. After showing improvement in first-to-second year retention between 2004 and 2006, it fell back to 2000 levels. In sum, the enrollment and retention initiatives failed to bring sustained gains.

For the first time, Ribeau lost some of the support of the Board of Trustees, which had been very strong for a decade. This is not an uncommon development in relations between presidents and trustees, reflecting to some extent the turnover of trustees and inevitable questions about the tenure of long-serving presidents. By 2004, the terms of all of the trustees who had appointed Ribeau had ended. One member of the Board of Trustees from an earlier era commented that as membership turns over, newer members often assume that the most influential role they can play is in selecting a new president. Whatever the causes, the Board became more assertive, playing a prominent role in the selections of Sherideen Stoll as the senior vice president for finance (formerly vice president for planning and budgeting) in 2006 and Shirley Baugher as provost in 2007.

In May 2008, Ribeau announced his resignation to become president of Howard University. As he departed, Ribeau won wide praise especially for his emphasis on "students first" and his community building. Two board members, Debra Ryan and William Primrose, spoke of his unique qualities. Ryan praised his "wonderful rapport with students ... [he] made them feel important ... [he] has a lot of respect from the faculty and staff as well." Primose, recalled, "The one thing I'll always remember about Sidney is when we went down to the GMAC Bowl [and] when he walked into the room all the kids stood up and applauded. They just love the man. That's so unusual on today's campuses that they just love the man."

Ribeau's leadership had changed Bowling Green. Michael Marsh, the Board's president during Ribeau's last year, described him as a "uniter [who] built community and made it possible for the whole University to move forward.

He makes everyone around him a better person." Kermit Stroh, a member of the Board of Trustees from 1993 to 2002 and co-chair of the Building Dreams campaign, praised Ribeau as "the premier president of any institution … He's just a great, great leader … In 1995, we were always saying 'We can't! We can't,' but with Ribeau it's always been 'We can! We can!'" David Bryan, Stroh's colleague on the Board of Trustees, called Ribeau "one of the best leaders I've worked with … an exceptionally good leader." Former provost Charles Middleton, now the president of Roosevelt University, said "Sidney Ribeau is a transformational president … BGSU is bigger, stronger, more reputable in 2008 than it was in 1995. He's one of the outstanding presidents in the United States."

Ribeau brought greater change to Bowling Green than any of his predecessors, with the possible exception of McDonald. Viewed in its entirety—from building community to the scholarship of engagement—the Ribeau presidency had a remarkable coherence, for each initiative led directly to the next. He enjoyed immense popularity and respect among students and staff. In informal conversations and before large groups, he was adept at articulating his vision for Bowling Green and conveying his enthusiasm for its realization.

Whether Ribeau's initiatives will survive depends on imponderables—future leadership, economic conditions, decisions in Columbus—but within a year of his departure financial constraints threatened his legacy in some ways. Springboard, one of the retention programs, was eliminated. The Partnership for Community Action and the Center for Innovative and Transformative Education were also terminated.

The "premier learning community" remains a worthy goal. A future president may define its characteristics differently, but Ribeau was correct in asserting the importance of having an ambitious vision. Whatever his shortcomings, Ribeau deserves credit for the dramatic change in Bowling Green's reputation as an undergraduate institution, for the emphasis on the highly successful private fundraising campaigns, and for the enhancement of the University's image externally and of morale internally.

Those were the worthy achievements of a transformative president. ■

Jerome Library: The 'Heart' of the University

When William T. Jerome returned to Bowling Green in 1983 for the ceremony that named "the library" in his honor, he said no recognition could be more meaningful, for a library was the "heart of any university." Until his death in 2008, Jerome took pride in Bowling Green's development, especially the library bearing his name.

BGSU's Music Library and Sound Recording Archives represent the largest collection of popular recorded music in an academic library in North America.

Since opening on June 19, 1968, the library has undergone many changes while expanding its holdings and services. The card catalogues have given way to online searches for materials available not only at Jerome Library, but at libraries throughout the state through Ohio LINK, a lending and borrowing system that creates in effect one gigantic library. The University also participates with the University of Toledo in the Northwest Ohio Regional Book Depository, located in Perrysburg, which holds important but rarely used materials, accessible on-site or through a daily delivery service.

Jerome Library has become widely known as a research center, which, beyond serving the needs of students and the public of northwest Ohio, attracts scholars from throughout the United States and beyond. The Center for Archival Collections (CAC) and the Browne Popular Culture Library (BPCL) both began modestly during the library's early years, but have grown into substantial research collections. The CAC was established in 1968 as the Northwest Ohio Great Lakes Research Center under Richard J. Wright of the history faculty, who brought to Bowling Green an extensive collection documenting the maritime history of the Great Lakes. Originally located in the former library, the center moved to Jerome Library in 1976 and the following year, it assumed responsibility for university archives and took its present name. The CAC under its archivists, Paul Yon, who later became director, and Ann Bowers undertook an extensive local records acquisition, which documents the political, cultural and economic history of northwest Ohio—one of the richest regional archives in the country. In addition, the CAC also administers the Rare Books and Special Collections.

The BPCL began in 1969 with a collection of books from Ray B. Browne, who was then starting the University's program in popular culture. His personal library of some 10,000 books has grown to some 190,000 books in addition to other materials, making BPCL the most extensive collection of its kind in the world. Individuals have contributed rich caches of popular materials. For instance, Arthur and Phyllis Rieser of New York City donated over 100 cartons of mystery books and David Lacey, a 1953 Bowling Green graduate, gave a large collection of "Hollywood books." The sound recording archive, accumulated by William Schurk, holds nearly one million recordings—the largest collection of popular records of any university library.

The BGSU Centennial

Bowling Green State University approached its Centennial confronting the "budget crisis of a century," but with a firm sense of direction. Much of that resolve can be traced to the leadership of Carol Cartwright, who was appointed interim president in July 2008.

Carol A. Cartwright agreed to taking the presidency after six months as interim president.

The Board of Trustees also named a Presidential Search Committee, but its work was terminated on Jan. 6, 2009 when Cartwright was named president for a three-year term.

The Board of Trustees' action paralleled a similar removal of "interim" from a presidential appointment to permit a more extended transition at a time of uncertainty. Similar to 1961 when Ralph Harshman's title was modified to facilitate recovery from the divisions of the Ralph McDonald controversy, the board's decision in 2009 reflected its conviction that stable leadership was needed in confronting the financial crisis. The problem of an "interim" president was reinforced when Shirley Baugher abruptly resigned as provost in December 2008, after a contentious 16 months in office, marked by faculty criticism of what many considered arbitrary policies driven principally by financial considerations. Also entering into the Board's calculation was the disappointing number of strong presidential applicants. Cartwright, who had been president of Kent State University from 1991 to 2006, responded hesitantly, but in the end favorably, to the board's overtures to eliminate "interim" from her title. When the board asked her for the third time to accept the presidency, she said that her "sense of duty really kicked in … I knew BGSU needed to send a strong signal that it had a fully engaged leader and was moving forward."

She demonstrated that same level of commitment and leadership during her presidency at Kent State. There she earned a reputation for firm leadership and an efficient "getting things done" administration. She was Kent State's 10th president and the first woman president of a state university in Ohio. Ironically she also became Bowling Green's 10th president and its first woman president. Prior to her career at Kent State, Cartwright, who earned her doctorate in education at the University of Pittsburgh, had been vice chancellor for academic affairs at the University of California at Davis and dean for undergraduate programs and vice provost at Pennsylvania State University.

Like Ribeau, Cartwright sought to build leadership beginning with human capital. In her early weeks, she spent much time visiting departments; she believed it was "essential to know people and programs and where they worked." She admired what her predecessor had accomplished, but at the same time she had the "100 percent responsibilities of the president" to confront a financial, enrollment and staffing situation that had steadily worsened. Indeed by the time that she took office, repeated budget cuts had taken their toll; there were few replacements for faculty or staff who left their positions.

Among the 24 faculty retirees in 2009 were three Distinguished Research Professors and two Ohio Eminent Scholars. The contracts of a number of experienced administrative staff were not renewed; financial aid lagged behind tuition increases; University revenue was reduced because fewer students were living on campus and buying meal plans, and the value of the endowment declined. It was as critical a situation as ever confronted the University's leadership.

Still when Cartwright delivered the State of the University address on Jan. 30, 2009, immediately following her brief inauguration, her message–"The Promise of Possibility"–was optimistic, talking about the University's role in economic recovery, the potential for the Centers of Excellence that were being established, and the capacity of the University "to think our way through [the budget crisis] in a very careful and organized way." She was especially buoyant about fulfilling the "mission that is committed to student success" and an ongoing conversation about the entire undergraduate experience. She said, "We will soon be able to present new students with a road map of all the requirements, opportunities and high-impact practices that will be made available to them. It will all add up to a world-class, coherent undergraduate experience." Cartwright closed by pledging "to share the power of engaging in change leadership–the power of thinking forward."

"Thinking forward" was called for in responding to the Ohio Board of Regents' mandate that each state university identify and build on "centers of excellence"–programs of national stature that could serve to attract investment and talent. Based on the recommendations of the Steering Committee on Interdisciplinary Themes, chaired by Milt Hakel, the University identified five such centers, most of which cross traditional disciplinary and collegiate lines:

» *Developing Effective Businesses and Organizations*

» *21st Century Education*

» *Health and Wellness Across the Lifespan*

» *The Arts*

» *Sustainability and the Environment*

"Thinking forward" was also evident in proposals, discussed throughout 2009, to reconfigure the academic area, in part to promote financial efficiency and to relate administrative organization to academic themes and objectives. In his first months in office, Kenneth W. Borland, whom Cartwright named senior vice president for academic affairs and provost, worked to coordinate this ambitious undertaking, the potential dimensions of which are without precedent in the University's history.

"Thinking forward" will be part of the ongoing discourse about the University's mission and the balance between the undergraduate and graduate/research objectives. In a way tension on that issue goes back to the attainment of university status in 1935, but it became more prominent during the presidencies of Ralph McDonald and William T. Jerome, who broke the "teacher college" mentality and built the early doctoral programs. Then Hollis Moore focused on undergraduate curricular reform. The presidencies of Paul Olscamp and Sidney Ribeau provided the most contrasts; the "new direction" of the former emphasized the graduate/research direction, while "the premier learning community" of the latter renewed the historic undergraduate mission. Bowling Green will likely continue to identify itself as "primarily an undergraduate institution, with focused graduate programs." The difficult part has always been in what that mission means in terms of evaluating academic units and allocating resources, which the program review of the Ribeau administration attempted to address.

Building Dreams: The Centennial Campaign for Bowling Green State University, the most successful private fundraising campaign in northwest Ohio at the time, played a big part in "Thinking Forward." When the campaign ended on December 31, 2008, it had received nearly $147 million in gifts and commitments, far surpassing the $120 million target that many had considered unattainable. The campaign received contributions from more than 70,000 alumni and friends, including 31 seven-figure gifts. Altogether, Building Dreams established 540 new scholarships, 13 endowed professorships and two endowed chairs. Among the principal projects was the previously mentioned Dallas-Hamilton Center for Entrepreneurial Leadership. The Sidney A. Ribeau President's Leadership Academy, as it was renamed by the Board of Trustees, was the beneficiary of a $6.7 million gift from Robert and Ellen Bowen Thompson to sponsor needy, inner-city students with leadership potential from the Detroit area.

Three major building projects also benefited; longtime donors provided substantial funding for the Sebo Athletic Center; the Wolfe Center for the Arts, located on the site of razed Saddlemire Student Services Building, and the Stroh Center, located in the former parking area to the east of the Mileti

46,533,152

More than $146 million was raised as part of BGSU's Building Dreams Centennial Campaign.

Alumni Center. Groundbreaking on the Wolfe Center and Stroh Center took place in 2009.

With leadership provided by a $1.5 million gift from Frederic and Mary Wolfe, benefactors of the arts in northwest Ohio, the Wolfe Center will "bridge" the arts with a glassed-in walkway across the building suggesting the connections with the nearby Fine Arts Center and Moore Musical Arts Center. A $750,000 gift from Thomas and Kathleen Donnell of Findlay supports construction of the main theatre. The Board of Trustees named the common space in front of the center the Ribeau Plaza.

Kermit F. Stroh and his late wife Mary Lu Stroh and their family donated $8.1 million—the largest single private gift in the University's history—primarily for the construction of the Stroh Center, a convocation-athletic facility that will provide a new home for the basketball and volleyball teams, with seating capacity of 5,000. Stroh, whose family has long connections to Bowling Green and who served on the Board of Trustees from 1993 to 2002, spoke of his vision of the center: "the one thing I hope is that the Stroh Center will be much more than just a basketball arena. I hope it will be able to facilitate events, activities and opportunities for the University and the greater community … for business gatherings, concerts and convocations. It will offer versatility for many different events."

William "Bill" Frack of Findlay, whose 60 years as a Falcons basketball fan began in 1948 when he was 12 and his father took him to a game in the "old men's gym" (Eppler South), provided a $2 million gift for the basketball court, which will bear his name. A $1.7 million gift from another devout longtime fan, Allen Schmidthorst and his wife Carol of Lima, will fund the Schmidthorst Pavilion team and practice space. Larry Miles of Findlay, class of 1956 provided a $1 million gift in memory of his late wife Joann (Schroeder) Miles, class of 1955, and late brother Lanny Miles, class of 1957, for a practice court "with a memory." The space, to be known as the "Court of Champions" will honor championship basketball and volleyball teams.

The construction of the Wolfe Center for the Arts and the Stroh Center mark the beginning stages of a building plan that will reconfigure the campus in ways comparable to the expansion of the 1950s and 1960s. In August 2009 the Board of Trustees approved a Residence and Dining Hall Master Plan and three months later, the first phase was announced. Two new residence halls are to be constructed by August 2011: one on the site of Rodgers Quadrangle and the Phi Kappa Tau and Sigma Phi Epsilon fraternity houses—all of which were razed—and the other in the parking area to the north of Offenhauer Towers. These will be the first new residence halls in 40 years. The moving of the fraternities also marks the first step toward the creation of a Greek Village that will cluster the houses of fraternities and sororities.

On the evening of April 25, 2009, a large gathering in the Lenhart Ballroom celebrated the Building Dreams Campaign. As the program ended, Kermit Stroh, as co-chair of the campaign, summoned the students to the front of the ballroom and led them in a rousing rendition of "Ay Ziggy Zoomba." Buoyed by the successful Building Dreams campaign and the spirit of "Ay Ziggy Zoomba," Bowling Green State University stood prepared for the challenges of its second century. ∎